Covert Surveillance Techniques

The Manual of Covert Surveillance Training

BY

PETER JENKINS

PUBLISHED BY

INTEL PUBLICATIONS

Covert Surveillance Techniques

The Manual of Covert Surveillance Training

1st Edition

Intel Publications
The Sett
Yate Lane
Oxenhope
Keighley
BD22 9HL
United Kingdom
www.charlieone.freeserve.co.uk

A CIP catalogue record is available from the British Library.

Printed and bound in Great Britain by:
Redwood Books, Trowbridge, Wiltshire.

Typesetting and Photographic Scanning: Protection Publications, Leeds.

Cover Design: Ian Gordon, Art Style, Leeds.

ISBN: 09535378 0 3

ACKNOWLEDGEMENTS

In preparation of this book, I would like to thank a number of people whose ideas, criticisms and support have been welcomed. In particular, Robert Armstead of DTS Investigations for his commitment to running the surveillance courses which urged me to complete this book. I am appreciative of Robert's help on some of the topics covered in this book and to whom I am very grateful.

Thanks to Ken Leak of X-14 Investigations for his constructive criticism during the draft stage. A long time friend and colleague with a wealth of experience and whose professionalism is second to none.

To Tony Priestley (L. Priestley Investigations) who gave me the break that I needed at the beginning.

From the military days, Chris Mawhood and John Napier, whose leadership and professional approach I was to respect and emulate.

Ian McQueen QGM at MAC Investigations for his valued comments and expertise.
John Daniel of Daniel Training Service.
Syd, Kate & Steve at Coast To Coast (Europe) Limited.
Direct Investigations (UK) - Hull.
Richard at All Seeing Eye Ltd.
Sean @ 2.S.I.
Dave Rayner, friend and fellow investigator.
Dave Allam at ASL.
Kathy Grigg - Thank you.

Callsigns: Bravo, Kilo, Romeo, Whisky, X-Ray, India, Mike and Charlie from 'Up North'. It's been a pleasure! - **DON'T POINT!!**

And to Peter Consterdine and Dawn at Chase Consultants Limited for their hard work and assistance in bringing this project to its conclusion. Thank you.

DEDICATION

To my Mother Marian who is so deeply missed,
My Father - Frank Jenkins
who taught me honesty and integrity,

And to the three beautiful ladies in my life,
Debra, Bethany and Kate.

C O N T E N T S

Introduction

The idea for this book came about when I first started as a Commercial Investigator almost ten years ago in 1990. At that time there were only a few books written on surveillance techniques which were American and slightly out of date. This book has taken a period of five years to complete and a draft copy has already been used as a training manual for surveillance courses that have taken place.

After 12 years service in the Royal Marines, I started my own business as a Commercial Investigator. Initially clients were very difficult to find and so the way forward was to freelance to other well established Private Investigation Agencies solely specialising in surveillance work.

It did not take long before I became busy with work from these Agencies. The reason for this increase in work load was due to the fact that many Private Investigators did not know how to carry out a surveillance effectively. They did not have the training, the experience or the correct equipment.

This statement is not meant to be derogatory to those agencies as they carry out other types of work other than surveillance such as statement taking, process serving, accident reports and tracing missing persons etc, and they do not necessarily specialise in the surveillance field. Many private investigators are retired policemen who may not have gained substantial surveillance experience during their careers. In addition, any person can set up in business as a private investigator without any formal training or qualifications.

Therefore this book is primarily aimed at the person who is new to surveillance and secondly to those who carry out surveillances and require a reference book. The order of topics bears in mind the fact that the reader is unlikely to have any prior knowledge of the subject. The introductory chapter provides an overview of the main areas of surveillance and then each chapter discusses the various techniques and equipment available to the surveillance operator.

Throughout the book certain 'surveillance vocabulary' is introduced and is used when necessary. There is a Glossary at the end of the book which maybe worth reading first.

This book is by no means complete. It is a teaching and reference book for Basic Covert Surveillance Techniques. There are many advanced techniques, items of equipment, radio procedures and subjects on 'counter surveillance' measures that have not been covered in this book. Although they were included in the original draft, it was decided after some consideration, that they should be omitted. It would be wrong to divulge all the 'trade secrets' as this could endanger individual operators and compromise surveillance operations that are currently being undertaken and likely to be carried out in the future.

Covert Surveillance is a means of gathering evidence and information. It is a skill, which when put to good use, can provide the investigator with vital information when other avenues have failed.

It therefore follows, that careful planning and preparation must take place beforehand and surveillance should not be entered into lightly. Any course of action taken during a surveillance could be made available to the defence as part of advance disclosure if it is a legal issue that you are investigating.

Surveillance can be either from a static point, on foot or from a vehicle. In most cases a combination of all three is usually the case with the Subject, (or target), even possibly taking public transport.

Everyone in the surveillance team has an important role to play, none less than the person who is actually watching the activity and reporting on it to the rest of the team. He or she are the eyes and ears of the surveillance and are in effect painting a picture. The more accurate the description the better the evidence and the better response from the team as a whole. The most important factor for any surveillance team is communication. Without any form of communication between the team members (i.e. radios) you will have no surveillance 'team'.

Surveillance work is not all excitement! Very often the amount of time spent waiting for something to happen far outweighs the amount of time that the subject is active. Long periods of boredom and frustration have to be overcome and this can only be achieved by personal discipline and experience. A mobile surveillance is not a 'mad car chase', driving at excessive speed whilst chasing the subject, but is carried out in a calm, relaxed, professional manner and most importantly, with self control.

This book illustrates the methods that experience and training have shown to be successful. It is not intended to replace practical exercises and experience, but has been compiled for use as a guide and reference book to the surveillance operative. I consider it sufficiently comprehensive to enable the investigator to plan, carry out, gather evidence and report on a covert surveillance. Various techniques are discussed, there is nothing 'special' about them and with some thought the reader will come to the conclusion that they are pure common sense when used in context.

Throughout the manual I have referred to the Surveillance Team and the Surveillance Operator. Within the Police, Military, Customs and other Agencies, surveillance teams of eight to twelve operators can be used at any one time. It is appreciated that in the Commercial Investigation environment there are restrictions in both cost and manpower and it may not be possible to use a 'complete' surveillance team. However, I consider a team of three operators to be sufficient for most tasks and it is a three man team that I have used as a base for the techniques and methods described in this book.

In the text, I have concentrated on surveillance techniques only and have deliberately missed out areas of investigation work such as 'background screening' and the various methods of obtaining information about a subject, as it is envisaged that the reader will already be familiar with these investigation procedures.

Much surveillance relies on the following of a subject by car and therefore the operators driving skills have to be first class. During a follow, there is a lot to think about which demands much concentration: the subjects movements and intentions, the giving of a radio commentary, directing the surveillance team, navigating and the recording of events, simultaneously whilst driving safely.

In the United Kingdom it is perfectly legal to carry out a surveillance, follow some-one and photograph them without their knowledge. There are laws concerning Trespass, Harassment and Stalking in this country of which the surveillance operator should be aware. These areas are not covered in this book but I would recommend that the novice surveillance operator should become familiar with them.

Should you find yourself working abroad, it would be recommended that you contact an investigator or the Police in the country concerned, regarding the law and surveillance. In some countries it is illegal to follow a person and in others it is illegal to even photograph someone without their knowledge or consent.

The surveillance operator is tasked to obtain evidence. This evidence is often used in legal proceedings and the operator may have to give evidence in court. The defence (or prosecution) may attempt to discredit you, your evidence and how it was obtained in order to assist their case. As a professional you must be credible and be able to justify your actions at all times.

The book is written in the male gender, this is purely for ease of writing. Although the profession is dominated by men, there are a number of very professional female surveillance operatives, who work on the security 'Circuit'.

Everyone charged with carrying out investigations and undertaking a surveillance in order to obtain evidence should find this book both informative and educational. Surveillance cannot be taught by reading a book alone. It is a practical subject that requires realistic training, practise and most of all experience. This book is a guide and reference to support that training and practice.

Peter Jenkins
Intel Security Services 1999

CHAPTER ONE

Covert Surveillance

In this first chapter we define the types and methods of surveillance, detail the qualities of a good surveillance operator and describe the areas which provide a grounding for the chapters to follow. First of all, what is a surveillance?

Definition

Surveillance is the continuous watching (Overt or Covert) of persons, vehicles, places or objects to obtain information concerning the activities and identities of individuals.

Objectives of a Surveillance

- To obtain evidence of a crime or unauthorised activity.
- To obtain detailed information about the subjects activities.
- To develop leads and information received from other sources.
- To know at all time the whereabouts of an individual.
- To confirm the reliability of informant information.

- To obtain information for later use in an interview.
- To locate persons (by watching their haunts and associates).
- To obtain information for search warrants.
- To obtain evidence for use in Court.

Types of Surveillance

Overt Surveillance

An open observation where we deliberately let the subject know that a surveillance is being conducted.

Covert Surveillance

A secretive watch where the subject is not aware of our presence.

Methods of Surveillance

Methods of surveillance can be conducted in various ways but are primarily divided into three groups. They can be conducted separately or a combination of all three.

- Static Surveillance
- Mobile Surveillance
- Technical Surveillance

Static Surveillance

Static Surveillance is where the surveillance operator(s) are in a static position from where they can keep observations such as: a building, hedgerow, surveillance vehicle, or by observing whilst on foot. Static Observation Posts (S.O.P.'s) may be divided into a further two groups - Urban and Rural O.P.'s depending on the local topography.

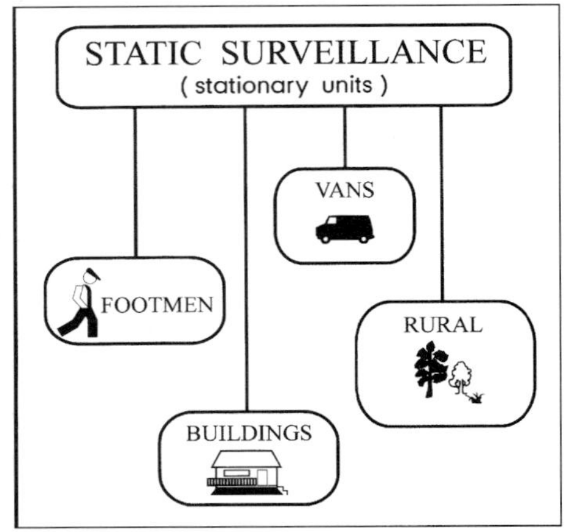

Static O.P's are used when the subject comes to your area of observation and you therefore await their arrival for them to be photographed (or whatever). The Static O.P. is also used as a 'trigger platform' to inform mobile operators that the subject is departing or arriving at the subject area. The different forms of Static O.P.'s are covered in detail in a later chapter.

Mobile Surveillance

Mobile Surveillance is when the operators act as mobile units and are used to follow moving subjects. The following of such subjects can be by car (or other motorised vehicle), motorbike, on foot or by boat.

Mobile techniques are used when the Subject has to be followed for whatever reason. Communication and radio voice procedure are vital to the success of a mobile surveillance. The mobile operators must be able to observe the Subject, provide radio commentary, navigate and record information simultaneously whilst also driving safely.

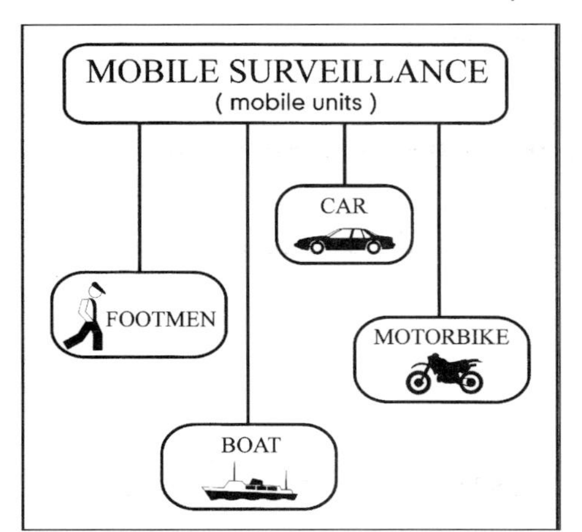

The operator must be flexible, and be prepared for ever changing situations such as the Subject leaving his car and proceeding on foot, using public transport or meeting with others.

Technical Surveillance

Technical Surveillance is a means of gathering information with technical devices such as room bugs/transmitters, tape recorders, telephone monitoring devices, video transmitters and vehicle tracking equipment. Each item will have its limitations, but used purposefully can be a very effective tool in gathering information and providing technical support to the other types of surveillance.

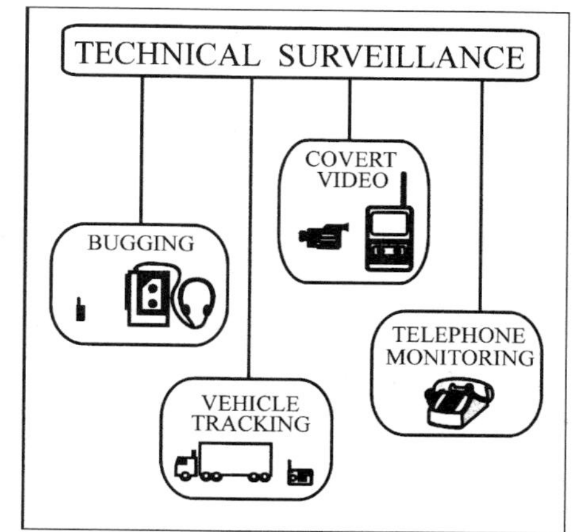

Technical Surveillance is a very specialised Subject and is therefore only briefly mentioned in this book. The various types of device and their uses can be found in the chapter on Equipment. Whilst it is perfectly legal to own and buy such surveillance devices, there are certain laws in the United Kingdom that may restrain the owner from using them.

THE SURVEILLANCE OPERATOR

A good standard of surveillance by an individual or team can only be acquired by training, practise and most of all, experience. It is important, not to stand out in a crowd and the operator should fit in with his surroundings. His dress code should suit the area in which he is operating and his vehicle should be given the same consideration.

The ideal surveillance operator could be described as:-

'Not too tall, too short, too fat or too thin, with no outstanding features, characteristics or mannerisms'.

And as being:-

A Mr. 'Nobody' but a Mr. 'Everybody' who looks like Mr. 'Average'.

Personal Qualities

The ideal surveillance operator must have the following qualities:

1. Be quick thinking and quick to react.
2. Be capable of acting naturally at all times and move unobtrusively.
3. Be able to fit and merge into a variety of backgrounds.
4. Have good eyesight and good hearing.
5. Have a good memory.
6. Be a good talker and actor.
7. Be physically fit.
8. Be able to work on his/her own initiative as well as part of a team.
9. Be a confident and proficient driver with good navigational skills.
10. Be astute to the local situation where he is working.
11. Be proficient in the use of all equipment such as cameras and radios.
12. Have a 'sixth sense', borne by experience.

During training courses, theory is practised in the classroom before going out on the ground.

Fitness

Ensure that you are fit and healthy enough to carry out the task. An operator out of breath with have difficulty communicating on the radio or keeping a camera steady. In addition, if you are full of cold it would not be suitable for you to operate in a static O.P. Coughs and sneezes could give away your presence and affect your performance.

Types of Subject Who Come Under Surveillance

Many people can be the Subject of a surveillance for many different reasons and can come from all walks of life. Listed below are three categories that the Subject may fall into.

Some 'hardened' targets may be totally unaware that they are being followed.

1. The person who disciplines and trains himself to look for 'watchers and 'followers' and who will carry out anti-surveillance tactics as a matter of course every time he appears in the open.

   This type of target is usually from the criminal element who has knowl edge of surveillance procedures or is a person who expects to be followed.

2. The person who does not consider or think about being watched or followed. This type of Subject can be very complacent about his activities and is easily caught out.

3. The person who expects to be followed or watched but does not know what he is looking for. This person will be alerted by noticing things that are out of the ordinary and unusual. They may adopt some anti-surveillance tactics.

Anti Surveillance Tactics

The person who expects to be followed will often carry out Anti Surveillance tactics and manoeuvres in order to identify any 'watchers' and to evade their surveillance.

In addition, a person who may suspect that he is being observed may carry out certain manoeuvres in order to confirm his suspicions that he is being followed.

Third Party Awareness

During a surveillance we are always conscious and concerned if the Subject becomes suspicious of our presence and actions. We must equally be aware of other unconnected people becoming suspicious of our presence. These unconnected persons we call **'Third Parties'** and we have to be aware of them more so than the Subject himself.

Third Parties could be innocent 'Neighbourhood Watch' residents or even criminals living in the same street as your Subject. Even so, you should be aware of anyone who is unconnected. It is the 'Third Party' that is more likely to call the police to report suspicious persons or vehicles in their neighbourhood. You maybe quite a distance from the Subjects house or premises (possibly acting as back-up to the trigger) but you still have to take precautions when deciding where to 'plot up'.

During a mobile or foot surveillance, act accordingly, never run or drive erratically and try not to be the focus of attention.

In order to minimise 'showing out' to third parties, adopt the following procedures:

- Be extremely observant to your surroundings when close to and away from your Subject.

- Be aware of Neighbourhood Watch Schemes.

- Keep all equipment such as radios and cameras out of view and covered up. This also applies to any paperwork, files or photographs.
- Be discrete when using the radio or a camera.
- Use the other team members to keep a look out if you have to do something you consider risky, i.e. photograph items in the rear of the Subjects vehicle or walk up a driveway etc.
- Adopt an identity - give yourself a purpose for being there.
- Have a convincing cover story ready if you are challenged by a member of the public.

Ensure that you have a cover story ready at all times. Provide a realistic excuse for your presence if challenged by a member of the public or the Subject himself. Curious neighbours will not tolerate excuses such as 'mind your own business'. This will arouse their suspicions further and they are likely to inform the Police.

> Never inform a member of the public that you are the Police or intimate that you are the Police. It is a criminal offence to impersonate a Police Officer.

Do you inform the Police of your presence and of the investigation?
There are many different trains of thought on this matter, both have their advantages and disadvantages but as a rule we do not usually inform the Police of our activities and this decision has been borne by past experience.

When working in 'rough areas' where there is a high risk of criminal element and the operators could be under threat, we would inform the local Police of our presence providing them of our vehicle details.

In the past we have provided the Police with our details when working in particular areas. Not long after being on the ground, a Police patrol car would arrive in the area searching and trying to spot us. This has happened on many occasions and does nothing to assist our cause but to alert the locals.

You will undoubtedly be stopped and questioned by the Police on occasions, therefore always carry some form of I.D card to prove to them that you are an investigator.

A 'Lost' Subject

Losing contact with the Subject of a surveillance is inevitable from time to time. The type of target who is expected to be followed will undoubtedly attempt to lose the tail.

Losses occur for many reasons, e.g. traffic congestion, busy roundabouts, traffic lights and lack of concentration. When this occurs the surveillance team must adopt a search pattern, (as described in a later chapter). It assists greatly if the operators draw on knowledge and background of the Subject in an effort to pick him up and continue the surveillance.

Never let over-enthusiasm of not wanting to lose the target result in 'showing out' and compromising the surveillance.

Being Compromised (Showing Out)

During any covert operation there is always the risk of 'showing out' and being compromised, experience and training will help to minimise this risk.

You will either show out personally, your vehicle will be noticed or it will be your actions that draw the Subjects attention. As an operator you will only have so many 'lives' and too much exposure will lose them one by one.

An experienced team member will know if he has been seen or noticed. Often we are very sensitive when the Subject looks in our direction and we are over cautious to the extent that we think we may have shown out. Should this be the case, you should make a quick decision whether the operator or team should pull out of the surveillance.

Be aware of the 'lost' driver. We have often followed drivers who appeared to be carrying out some sort of anti-surveillance manoeuvres when in fact they were only lost and so kept driving up and down the same stretch of road trying to locate a premises.

If you feel that you may lose contact with the Subject, and by keeping close you risk showing out, then it is better to let him continue and experience a loss. Remember

> There is always another day.

PRINCIPLES OF A SURVEILLANCE

Principle Stages

The actual surveillance can be broken down into the following three stages:

- The Trigger
- The Follow
- Housing

The Trigger

The start of the surveillance can be the most difficult and critical part and is known as the 'Trigger'. The whole operation can go wrong at the outset if the Subject is not able to be 'triggered' away from his house or premises. It is the task of the trigger man to keep the Subject house or premises under observation in order to alert the remainder of the team when the Subject departs.

There are three types of Trigger to consider:

- Static Trigger
- Mobile Trigger
- Technical Trigger

Static Trigger

The trigger 'platform' can be from a car (overtly), a van, building, hedgerow or any other static point from where the Subjects premises can be covertly observed from. During this phase the trigger man plays the most important role in the team, he has to be alert at all times and have total concentration on the Subject premises.

At the first sign of possible movement by the Subject, the trigger man puts the team on 'Standby'. He should provide the team with a radio commentary of the Subject's actions such as getting into a vehicle or any other activity. He should also state the Subject's intended route, the route being taken and give a description of the Subject and what he is wearing.

If the Subject's premises cannot be observed, you may have to place the trigger on the first road junction on the approaches.

This is probably the most crucial part of a surveillance, especially if you have no knowledge of the Subject or his intended movements. A Subject is likely to know short cuts and back street routes in the local vicinity to his house and may well take them to avoid heavy traffic etc. Therefore the Subject is more at risk of being 'lost' in the first few minutes of the surveillance than at any other time.

Mobile Trigger

If, for a number of reasons, the Subject premises are not able to be kept under static observation you will not be able to provide a static trigger. This situation normally occurs when a mobile Subject stops somewhere unexpectedly or stops in a cul de sac of a housing estate or industrial estate etc.

The only option open to you would be to place an operator at each possible exit of the route that the Subject may take on his departure. If the options are many, the team leader should decide on which exit most likely to be taken. All the team members should know the whereabouts of their colleagues and the exits that they are covering.

In this instance the operator has to be alert and observant at all times, as the Subject may be travelling at speed or suddenly depart in a different vehicle. Once the Subject has been identified as being mobile, the other team members should be informed immediately to ensure that they close up and continue the surveillance.

Technical Trigger

Electronic devices may be utilised to provide a trigger to alert the team that the Subject is going mobile. These technical triggers can either be audio or video operated.

- **Audio Trigger**

A simple audio transmitter can be covertly placed in the Subject area (such as a garden hedgerow), in order for you to listen (via a receiver) to what is happening in the area, such as doors opening/closing and vehicle engines starting.

> *On one occasion we had to trigger a Subject out of a block of flats where we could not observe the front doors or the car park. A cheap VHF transmitter was concealed in the foyer of the flats which transmitted the sound of people walking down the stairs and using the main doors. We were able to listen in and put the team on 'standby' every time we heard the door slam shut. This provided us with the extra time we needed to put a footman in position to cover the exit, in order to check and confirm the Subject leaving.*

A similar system can be used whereby a signal being transmitted to a receiver will warn of a vehicle being started. The device is covertly attached to the underside of a vehicle by magnets, where it remains dormant until the vibration of the starting engine switches it on and activates a transmitter. The transmitted signal is received on a unit (held by an operator) which gives a beeping tone when activated. The operator can then put the surveillance team on standby and await the target going 'mobile'.

- **Video Trigger**

A video camera located in a hedgerow or concealed in a car and pointing at the Subject, can transmit video pictures by UHF/VHF or Microwave signals. An operator, (located nearby in a safe area) can trigger the surveillance by watching the Subject area on a small television monitor. When activity is viewed on the screen, the team can be put on standby. The camera will be able to tell you what direction the Subject is travelling in and possibly what he is wearing and any other relevant details.

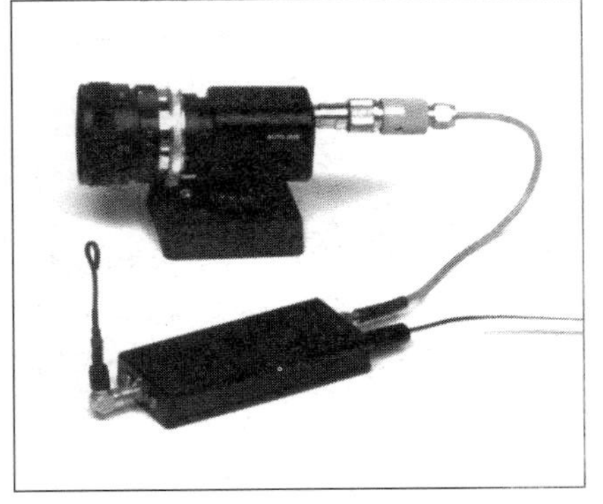

Covert, miniaturised and transmitting video camera.

These devices are not very expensive and can be used to good effect when other conventional means fail or are considered too risky.

The Follow

The Follow is the term used when the Subject is 'mobile' and has left the 'trigger' or 'pick up' point. At this stage you know where the Subject is and the team can be deployed to the best advantage.

The surveillance team has to work as a 'team' whether they are following by car or on foot and the techniques are discussed in the relevant chapters.

Housing

Housing the Subject after a follow can often be the most difficult part of any surveillance and could be the most important. By identifying the address or premises that the Subject enters, it may provide that final, vital piece of information you have been waiting for.

You may have observed the Subject for many days but he now suddenly arrives and parks his vehicle in an unknown street. It is imperative that an operator is close enough to identify the property that he enters and may possibly mean deploying an operator on foot as quickly as possible to identify the address.

When the Subject comes to a stop, an operator needs to be in close, in order to identify the premises that he has entered.

> During a surveillance the Subject's direction of travel (whether on foot or mobile), must always be given as 'Left', 'Right', or 'Straight'.
>
> These directions are always in relation to the SUBJECT'S 'Left' or 'Right' and not yours as you look at him.

CHAPTER TWO

2

Planning & Preparation

> PERGE SED CAUTE
>
> *Proceed With Caution*
>
> *Author's Family Motto*

Detailed planning and preparation should be carried out prior to a surveillance and is essential in order for it to succeed.

> Prior Planning and Preparation Prevents Poor Performance

Is Surveillance the Solution?

When obtaining your brief, decide whether or not surveillance would provide the answer to your clients problem. There are many reasons why a surveillance should be carried out but could the answers to your investigation be found out by other means?

Pretext telephone calls, visits to neighbours, or even speaking to the Subject of inquiry on a pretext can often lead to the results that you require. In addition, covert video cameras or controlled audio monitoring may provide you with information that you can act upon, without having to resort to lengthy and costly surveillance.

The Surveillance Option

Considering that surveillance is the option that you have decided to take, you will require as much information as possible from the client concerning the Subject of enquiry and the circumstances with which to formulate a plan.

It is essential that you establish whether the Subject has been under surveillance in the past. It will affect how you conduct your own surveillance.

The planner should decide the aims of the surveillance and then work in a methodical approach to arrive at a viable plan. Regardless of whether the task is a simple short one man affair, or a complex team task requiring the use of static and mobile operators; all require some form of detailed planning.

The Subject

As much information about the Subject is needed and this can be provided by the client or by your own investigations. Points to consider are:-

- Subjects name, nick-name or aliases
- His address and associated addresses.
- Telephone number.
- Description: age, build, height, hair, clothing, features etc.
- Is a photograph or video available of him?
- Type of vehicle: make, model, colour, registration.
- Other occupants of the household.
- Job: workplace, hours, shifts, method of travel, routines.
- If unemployed, day, time and place he signs on for unemployment benefit.
- Habits: smoker, pubs, clubs, friends or associates, activities.

Sources of information can be obtained from:-

- The Clients Brief
- A pretext visit to the Subjects address to identify him
- Telephone Directories
- Trade Directories
- Electoral Register
- County Courts Register
- On Line Computer Searches
- Companies House
- Local Enquiries
- Informants.

PRE-SURVEILLANCE REPORT

Prior to any surveillance being carried out a reconnaissance visit should be made of the Subject locations, the target area should be visited to enable you to plan and organise the task. This could be residential, business premises or an area in which the Subject is going to be or likely to visit.

You will carry out a pre-surveillance (Recce) in order to establish how the surveillance is to be run, manpower, where to observe from, positions for the team members and any likely hazards etc.

A pre-surveillance check list is found below, detailing the factors that should be known or considered and is then discussed in detail.

PRE-SURVEILLANCE CHECK LIST

Subject address/location: ______________________________
____

Approach and Route: ______________________________
____

Recce 360 degrees from Subject premises considering:-

How many observation positions are available and their locations.

FACTORS TO BE CONSIDERED

Routes in/out to O.P and drop off points
Can you see the target clearly
Can you observe the approaches - all routes in and out
Are you overlooked
Can the target see you/Is it obvious
Position for back up & support units
Radio check to back up
Position of Emergency R.V
How long to establish (E.T.A)
Note any particular hazards
Observation rest area, meals, toilet facilities
Special equipment & aids
Team base accommodation
Additional Information

PRE-SURVEILLANCE REPORT

In detail we look at each heading in turn and discuss:-

Subject Address/Location

Ensure the address is correct and provide a description of it, especially if it is difficult to locate. If there is no number on the door - double check. Draw a sketch plan of the immediate area indicating all routes in and out by vehicle or on foot.

Identify possible O.P. locations to trigger the surveillance and 'lie up' positions for the back-up units.

Approach and Route

Operators may have to make their own way to the Subject's location rather than be led there by the team leader. Directions should be taken from a main local landmark to the premises or to a central R.V point. Obtain Local Street and Ordnance Survey maps and consider the use of aerial photographs if necessary.

Recce 360 Degrees

Carry out a recce 360 degrees surrounding the Subject premises (do not just consider the front of the premises, there may be hidden access to the rear) consider how many observation positions are available and their locations. Remember, the O.P position could be in a van, car, hedgerow or building etc.

A Cul-de-Sac with nowhere to park without being obvious is often overcome by watching the first junction.

The following factors should be considered when choosing your O.P location:

Route In and Out

The route in and out of the O.P should provide you with easy access and be covered from view of the Subject if possible. The route in does not always have to be the same route out and consider Third Parties. Identify areas where the O.P. team may have to be dropped off and picked up by vehicle.

Can you see the Subject?

Once in the O.P. you should be able to see the Subject clearly. Should the target premises cover a large area you should have a good field of view or even consider using two or more O.P.s to observe it. Consider whether your field of view will become obstructed by passing or parked vehicles etc.

Can you observe the approaches?

The approaches to the Subject should be able to be observed. This will assist when waiting for a Subject to arrive and give you that extra time you may need to have cameras up and running. On the Subjects departure you may need to inform the team of his leaving, giving his direction of travel. In addition you need to see the approaches to your O.P. in the event of a 'Third Party' approaching. All routes at the rear of the premises should be assessed in the event the Subject departs on foot.

Are you overlooked?

Should the O.P be in a built up area, be aware of anyone above you in buildings or offices. Likewise should you be in a rural situation, be aware of anyone on high ground who may be able to look down onto your position.

Can the target see you?

Is your O.P in an obvious position? You do not want the O.P to be in a position that will attract attention. If it is in an isolated position it may arouse curiosity.

Position for Back Up & Support

A suitable position should be found where your back-up and mobile units can be located. The position should be close to the O.P. so the back-up can assist you if compromised and can reach you quickly. The position has to be within radio range and should not attract attention from 'third parties'.

Emergency Rendezvous

An emergency rendezvous (ERV) should be located and known by the surveillance team. In the event the O.P. is compromised or the surveillance team is split up, they can make their own way to the ERV to reorganise themselves and plan what action to take next.

How long to Establish

Estimate how long it will take to move into position and establish the O.P. to commence observations. This will effect your timings when planning the insertion. It could be a simple affair of driving a surveillance van into position or having to navigate across country, and then set up a hide in a rural O.P.

Particular Hazards

Note any particular hazards that may present themselves such as:-
parking problems, traffic conditions, security patrols, neighbourhood watch, wildlife and animals, floodlighting at night, CCTV cameras etc.

Be aware of the 'Third Party'. You are more likely to be noticed by them than by the subject.

Rest Area, Meals, Toilet Facilities

Depending on how long your surveillance is going to be you may require an area where you can rest, eat and go to the toilet within the confines of the O.P. In addition, the back-up and mobile units will also require these facilities.

Special Equipment & Aids

Decide what special equipment or aids you may need for the surveillance. Equipment such as tripods, powerful lenses, night vision scopes, electronic devices or camouflage nets will need to be considered.

Team Base Accommodation

Should the team be staying in the vicinity of the target area for a number of days then a suitable hotel or other accommodation should be found. When choosing a hotel consider the fact that you may be getting up fairly early in the mornings and that your comings and goings may appear suspicious to the staff. Motorway hotels and Travel Lodge type hotels are convenient and offer privacy.

Additional Information

Add any relevant information that you think is necessary such as sighting of any suspects, any vehicles noted at the time and whether a pretext visit was made etc.

On one occasion we carried out a recce for a task where the main gate and security lodge of a large company had to be kept under surveillance. This company was situated in a very large modern industrial estate where mounds of earth had been created to provide 'natural' divisions between the boundaries and were covered in bushes and small trees. It was our intention to put a rural O.P. in the foliage from where we could observe the main gate and security lodge.

Two of us went on the recce quite overtly, suitably attired as 'Highway Maintenance' workers, armed with petrol strimmers and the intention of clearing away over grown grass at the side of the road etc. Whilst one was able to get a close look at the subject area and create a diversion with the strimmer, the other was able to identify an O.P. position and create a hide in the foliage. A string line was then laid to enable us to follow it in the dark which led us into the O.P. position.

In the following three nights we were able to move into the position and carry out the surveillance without any difficulties.

Rural O.P.s do not necessarily have to be in the countryside. The rural O.P. could be used in this 'modern urban', industrial park.

Failing to Plan is Planning to Fail

Ref: PCL/422

RECCE REPORT

C/S Romeo
1530hrs 5/11/98

A1: Michael JONES
Description:-Age 51yrs, grey hair, overweight, spectacles

B1: Red VW Golf Reg: **R123 ABC** ***T.B.C.***

C1: 6 Manor Close, Cullingworth, Nr Bradford, BD20 1AZ. Tel: Ex-D.

A-Z O.S. West Yorkshire Page 52, D/5. O.S. Grid 068363

Route M62 (jcn 24), A629 (N) via Elland, Halifax, Denholme for 11 miles.Right at the 3 Flags Hotel onto B6429, Right at mini-roundabout, 1st right is Manor Close.

R.V. 3 Flags Hotel Car Park.

Area Small neat estate of private houses. Cars are parked on the roadside as well as private driveways. Manor Close is formed in a loop, giving two possible exits to the main Bradford Road.

There is only one foxtrot route (Public path between houses 2 & 4). Would only expect A1 to use this route if walking a dog etc.

Area is Neighbourhood Watch, therefore drive pasts will be restricted.

There is a small shop and a pub within walking distance, left of C1.

C1: C1 is the third property on the right as you enter the estate. It is the only house with a black satellite dish to the front and has a white porch to the front. To the side is a car port for one vehicle fronted by an iron gate.

There is no access to the rear from the rear.

Escape Routes: The two main mobile exits and the foxtrot route only.

Bravos: Red VW Golf (R123 ABC) static on drive. May require a late night visit to identify any others.

Trigger: Trigger can be given from van position marked on sketch (layby parking area opposite C1). To be inserted, can self extract if positioned carefully beside hedge.

Back Up: There are many locations for mobile units to lie up safely and cover the two exits on a 'Standby'.

Sightings: No sighting of subject at time of recce.

Misc: A car will have to be inserted into the trigger position on the night prior to the surveillance to 'reserve' a space as parking on the morning may be difficult. Electoral Register lists Michael and Hannah Jones only.

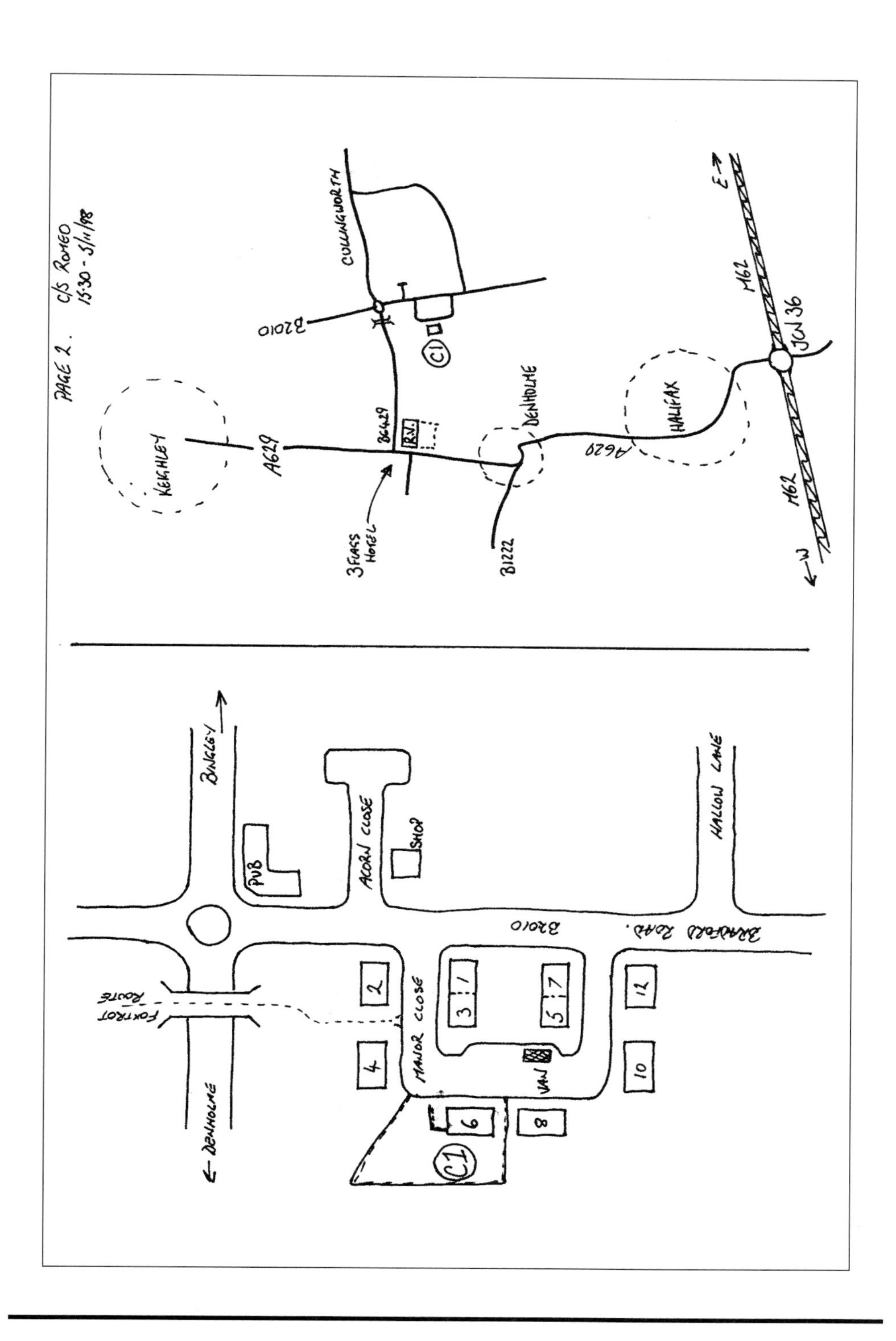
PAGE 2.
C/S ROMEO
15:30 - 5/11/98
KEIGHLEY
A629
B6429
R.J.
3FLAGS HOTEL
B2010
C1
CULLINGWORTH
DENHOLME
B1222
A629
HALIFAX
JCN 36
M62
M62
E
W
BINGLEY
PUB
ACORN CLOSE
SHOP
HALLOW LANE
B2010
BRADFORD ROAD.
FOXTROT ROUTE
DENHOLME
MANOR CLOSE
VAN
C1
1
2
3
4
5
6
7
8
10
12

The Plan

On completion of the recce, you will have to formulate a plan of action in order to carry out the task, within the bounds or restrictions placed on you by the client. Points to consider are:-

- The size of the Surveillance team.
- The make up of the team, males or females or both.
- Team vehicles, such as cars, vans, motorbikes etc.
- Any specialist equipment required.
- Calculate the man hours to provide an estimate of costs.

Blocks of flats can be a problem. It is essential to identify the Subject or his car at the planning stage.

EXERCISE

Consider the sketch plan below. You require to put a surveillance on the Subject's house in order to observe him load his vehicle with goods, watch him depart and then follow him to his destination. You have at your disposal 4 Operators with radios, you have between you 1 Surveillance van and 2 Cars.

Decide where you would place your operatives in order to trigger the surveillance and follow him away. List the advantages and disadvantages of your considered options. The Subject will have to be triggered out of the house, observed loading his car and then followed.

It is known that the suspect drives a car which is usually parked in the cul de sac, and he leaves home at about 08.25hrs every morning.

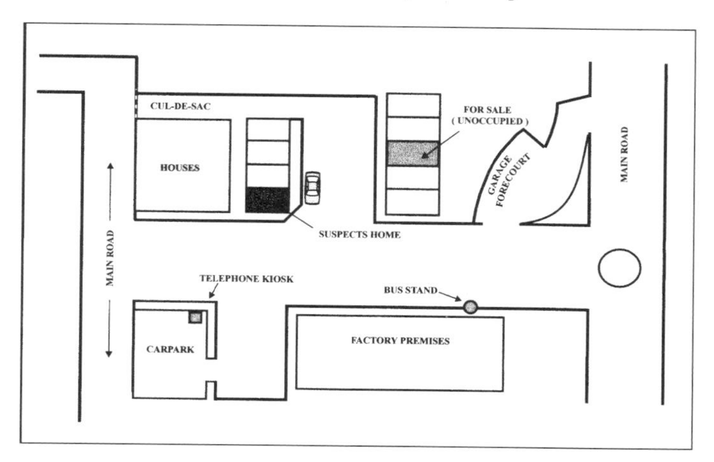

Considerations

Observation Positions for the 'Static Trigger'

Surveillance Van

- **Positioned in cul-de-sac** will provide the Eyeball of the suspect getting into his car. Positioned directly outside the house for sale will give a good overall view. Third Parties may connect the presence of the van with the house. Positioned in the Mill Staff Car Park may be suitable but be aware of company personnel being suspicious.

Operator on foot

- **Located in telephone kiosk**, you will be able to observe the front of the house but only for a short term.

- **Located at the bus stop**, again, you will be able to observe the front of the house but only for a short period, no longer than 20-30 minutes per operator, or depending on how frequent the buses are.

- **Located in the factory premises**, you will be able to overlook the property and the approaches. If you have to approach the factory manager do so as a last resort. The suspect may know people at the factory or have family working there.

• **Located in the unoccupied house for sale**. You would be able to observe the house and the approaches. You must decide whether to approach the Estate Agents and tell them of your intentions. If permission is granted, consider whether you leave the operator in situ when the Subject goes 'mobile' or will he have to be picked up by a team member? Alternately, is he better off remaining in position for the Subjects return? Consider the neighbours noticing something out of the ordinary with people coming and going from the house etc.

Positions for the Mobile Units

• **Factory Car Park.** In this position the operator can quickly move into a position to follow the Subject as he leaves the cul de sac. The car will be parked between other cars and therefore be covered from view. Be aware of observers from the factory who may over look you.

• **Garage Forecourt** This could be a viable option as it covers a route onto the roundabout and could be only used short term. Be aware of the garage proprietor, he may know the Subject.

• **Main Road on Left** This could be busy with traffic at 08.30hrs and the Subject has a choice of turning in two directions. If his route is known, mobile units could be deployed to pick him up after he has departed.

• **Mini Roundabout on Right** Again, this could be busy with traffic and visibility difficult. If this route is known, it may be considered putting a unit on an exit road from the roundabout. If a van is used to trigger the Subject, both mobile operators can be located on the main roads and can draw closer on a 'standby'.

Conclusion

The above points are very general and there is no text book answer but we have dealt with particular situations that can possibly arise. The initial point to consider is 'how many operators are available to me?' Once this is known you can then weigh up all the options of where to place your units to the best advantage.

It is essential that a recce is carried out at the Subject's address and that as much information is obtained about him in order to plan and carry out a successful surveillance.

Knowledge, Grounded on Accuracy,

Aided by Labour,

And Prompted by Perseverance,

Will finally overcome all Difficulties.

Ancient Charge

CHAPTER THREE

Observation Skills

In this chapter we look at various aspects which help us to notice events, recognise and describe people.

Subject Detail

On arrival at the Subject address, make a note of the surrounding details. Should you be keeping a house under surveillance, it is possible that you may not see any sign of life for many hours.

This can be disheartening for the investigator and puts doubt that there is anyone at home. The Subject could be a late riser or he could have left home prior to you arriving.

Rather than make a pretext visit or phone call to the house, which may alert the subject, your powers of observation will tell you if anyone is present. Things to look out for are:-

- The state of the curtains and windows - have they changed?
- Are there any lights on?
- Chimney smoke
- Milk on the doorstep
- Cats waiting to be let in or dogs barking
- Steam from bathroom window or vents
- Birds flying off when disturbed
- Noise from machinery such as tools or lawnmowers etc.

Consider delivering a circular or a newspaper by placing it half way into the letterbox. Should it be taken in, you will know that someone is up and about.

You may not always be in a position to observe any of the doors and so any of the above indicators will tell you that someone is present and may give you prior warning of them leaving.

Should there be two exits from the property (e.g. a house), you may have to put a 'trigger' on each. Alternatively, consider putting some sort of 'tell tale' marker on the rear gate/door that will be disturbed if it is used.

In addition to being visually aware, you should also rely on your hearing. You may probably hear the sound of doors and gates opening, car alarms being unset etc. This will give you those extra seconds of warning to have your camera up and ready or to put the surveillance team on standby.

DESCRIBING PEOPLE

It is not always possible to obtain a photograph of your Subject and so a full description of him should be taken from those instructing you, so that he is immediately recognisable.

Photographs of Subjects

Whenever possible obtain photographs or video of your Subject. Obviously, the more recent the picture the better and establish whether your Subject has changed since it was taken, i.e. grown a moustache, now wears glasses or has dyed his hair etc. Do not pay lip service to identification photographs, study them and examine facial detail and bodily details so that the Subject is instantly recognisable when seen for the first time.

Sometime comparisons can be difficult so carry the photograph with you on the task and use it. There is no point in having a photograph if it is going to be left at the office!

The description details you will require are:-

- Sex
- Ethnic Origin
- Age
- Height
- Build and Weight
- Hair - style, length, colour
- Features - shape of face
- Facial Hair
- Spectacles or jewellery
- Tattoos, scarring or blemishes.
- Speech (accent)
- Gait
- Clothing
- Resemblances
- Overall Appearance

Quite often you will have to describe certain persons in your reports. Even if you recognise your Subject from a photograph, it is always wise to add a description of that person to your log or report. The descriptive list shown above should be sufficient for most purposes.

Characteristics and features vary and could be describe in the following ways:-

ETHNIC ORIGIN

Your description of origin should be treated as being descriptive rather than a guess. Terms to be used could be: White, Negro, Asian, Arabic, Hispanic, Oriental, Latin, Scandinavian, East European etc.

AGE

To estimate age, compare the Subject's age with your own or someone that you know. If you find this difficult, try to 'bracket' their age, i.e. if you feel that they can not be older than 50 but are not as young as 40, we can estimate that the Subject is approximately 45 years old.

HEIGHT

Height can be estimated in a similar manner as we would for ages. Compare the Subjects height to yourself or someone you know and bracket accordingly. In addition, you can compare the Subject against his surroundings such as a door frame or a car roof etc. Height can sometimes be difficult to estimate as the persons build can often alter our perception.

BUILD

Describing build could be considered as:- Slim, Medium, Heavy, Well Built, Proportionate, Stout, Stooped, Small, Athletic, Muscular and Wiry.

HAIR

Hair can be described in many ways but we divide hair styles into three categories:-

- **Colour** Light, Dark, Fair, Streaked, Bleached, Tinted, Coloured, Black, Brown, Grey etc.
- **Length** Cropped, Short, Balding, Collar Length, Shoulder Length, Long etc.
- **Style** Tidy, Scruffy, Wavy, Permed, Straight, Thick, Thin, Curly, Receeding, Greasy, Fringed, Styled, Spiky, Bob etc.

FACIAL FEATURES

- **Complexion**

  Pale, fair, tanned, olive, rashy, weathered, dark etc

- **Shape of Face**

  When looking at faces there are many features that make up the face apart from the overall shape.

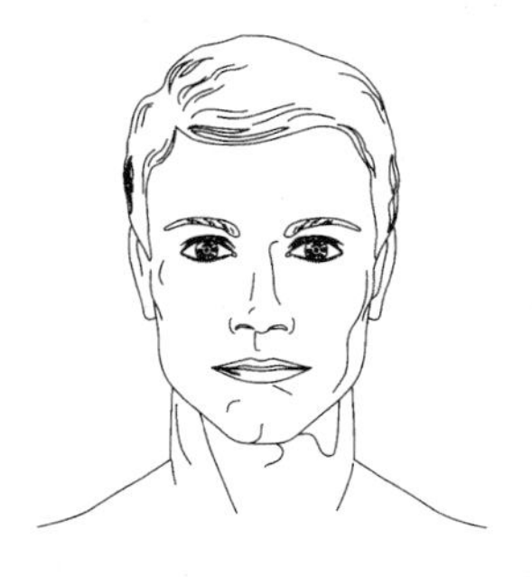

Facial shapes could be described as: - Round, Fat, Thin, Pointed, Angular, Square, Oval, Sallow, Small.

Eyes

Large, Small, Squint, Slanted, Bloodshot, Piggy, Piercing, Hooded Lids, Wide.

Eyebrows

Thick, Thin, Bushy, Arched, Plucked, Narrow, Joined, Slanted, Straight.

Noses

Small, Large, Button, Hooked, Roman, Fat, Bumpy, Snub, Bulbous, Wide, Pointed, Squashed.

Chins

Square, Round, Pointed, Long, Double, Angular.

Facial Hair

- **Moustaches:** Military, Droopy, Handlebar, Bushy/Thick, Toothbrush, Mexican, Thin, Walrus, Clipped, Waxed.

- **Beards:** Stubbly, Unshaven, Pointed, Long, Straggly, Short, Designer.

Spectacles and Jewellery

- **Spectacles:** Round, Square, Horn Rimmed, Metallic, Bi-Focal, Tinted.

- **Jewellery:** Rings, Necklaces, Medallions, Broaches, Earrings, Hairslides.

Tattoos

Obtain the design of the tattoo and their locations. Tattoos are designed for showing off and are often found on the forearms.

Speech

Regional accents are not always distinct but attempt to put the accent to an area, even if it is only North, South, Midland or West Country etc. Consider the tone and volume such as quiet, soft, loud, slurred, educated, clipped etc.

Gait, Stride and Posture

Most people have an identifiable gait in the way they hold themselves and move whilst walking.

- **Posture/Bearing:** Upright, Slouched, Stooped, Round Shouldered, Head Drooped, Lethargic.
- **Gait and Pace:** Fast, Slow, Bouncy, Marching, Skipping, Plodding, Springy, Dainty, Lethargic, Limping.

Clothing

Smart, scruffy, casual, business like, sporty, industrial.

Overall Appearance

Smart, Tidy, Untidy, Professional, Scruffy, Casual.

Resemblances

Does the Subject resemble anyone famous, such as a T.V. personality etc.

Mick Jagger

On one particular investigation, we were tasked to establish that a particular character worked in a busy car garage and obtain photographs or video of him working there. The client did not have very good powers of description but stated that the Subject looked very similar in appearance to the entertainer Bruce Forsyth, by having a long prominent chin.

On arrival at the garage, there were approximately 16 male staff working there and the Subject was instantly recognised. Should we not have had this descriptive 'resemblance' our task would have been made much more difficult by having to ask pretence questions etc.

VEHICLE DETAILS

Any vehicle details that you can obtain regarding the Subject are extremely useful. When vehicles arrive on the scene of an observation, or you arrive there to find a vehicle for that matter, it is important that you record as much detail as possible about it.

Make and Model: The make could be either a Ford or a Vauxhall, the Models possibly being an Escort or Astra respectively. In addition, there are variants such as Estates, Saloons or Hatchbacks. If you do not know what make it is, provide a detailed description.

Colours are fairly straight forward with variants in shades and metallic finishes. Make a note of the state of repair and body work, does it have any modifications? Registration numbers are unique to every vehicle and are the best means of recognition.

Note any unusual markings or ornaments such as stickers, furry dice, nodding dogs, tow bars etc. In busy traffic you may only get a brief sighting of a sticker in a rear window when the car is way ahead of you, this may be the only indicator to provide its location in a long queue of traffic.

Remember, if the Subject drives a powerful car, it may be necessary for the surveillance team to use similar powered vehicles also.

A small chalk mark, or a pebble can be used to indicate whether a vehicle has been moved whilst unobserved.

On occasions it may be necessary to identify whether a car or vehicle has remained parked in the same position overnight without moving. In order to do this, place a small chalk mark on the ground and also on the tyre so that they are in line with each other. In the morning you can casually walk past and examine the marks, if the two chalk I marks are not aligned it would indicate that the vehicle has been moved during the night.

Alternatively, place a small pebble on top of a tyre. If it is still there the following morning you know that the vehicle has not been moved.

NIGHT VISION

After being in a well lit area and moving into the dark, it takes about 20 minutes for your eyes to get accustomed to the dark and about 40 minutes to become fully adjusted. This adjustment is what we call night vision or 'getting used to the dark'.

At the back of the eye is the retina which is made up of cells, these cells (of which there are two types) are formed in the shape of rods and cones. The cones are sensitive to coloured light but not shades of grey. Alternately, the rods are not sensitive to colours but are to shades of grey. During the daytime, the cone cells are used to transmit light to the brain, as darkness takes over so do the rods.

When we go from one extreme to another such as light to dark, it takes some time for the cells to change role and so we have this 20-40 minute period of 'getting used to the dark'.

The suggestion that carrots help you to 'see in the dark' is true to some extent. Carrots are rich in Vitamin 'A' and it is known that Vitamin 'A' stimulates the cells that we have mentioned.

Once night vision is obtained, it is easy to lose it again by looking at bright lights or through night vision scopes, therefore when observing at night consider the following:-

- Scan areas of observation slowly.

- Do not look directly at the object, the eye has a 'blind spot' so look slightly to one side.

- Do not stare at an object, your eyes will play tricks on you. Avoid looking at bright lights, this will ruin your night vision.

- Keep your eyes closed when exposed to light such as car headlamps etc. If necessary, keep one eye open.

- Rest your eyes frequently.

- Looking through a night vision scope can ruin your night vision.

Soldiers preparing to carry out night time operations (such as going into a night assault by helicopter) will often sit for 40 minutes in darkness to enable their eyes to become accustomed to the dark. The troops may wait in a special area or all the lights inside the aircraft may be switched off.

Red light does not affect night vision so some illumination in these areas help you to see.

CHAPTER FOUR

Communications

Communications are probably the most important factor when there is more than one investigator working on the same task. Team tasks can succeed or fail depending on whether good communication is maintained between the team members and that those team members are well exercised in voice procedure and the giving of a radio commentary.

Communication is about being able to speak or indicate to another, in a manner that is **clear, precise, detailed** and **understandable** to the receiving party. In this instance, the sender will be passing information about a particular Subjects actions and intentions, or be issuing instructions to the remainder of the surveillance team.

Communication, (or Comms), can passed in any of the following ways:

- The telephone, including mobile phones.
- Radio transmissions.
- Hand signals

The Telephone

Mobile telephones are not recommended as a substitute for hand held radios. The cost of operating a mobile phone is probably one of the first disadvantages that springs to mind, but mobile networks can be very temperamental and calls have a habit of suddenly being cut off. If you are operating in a hilly or 'bad area' you will have no Comms. at all.

The obvious advantage is that they have an unlimited range of transmission where you can get in touch with anyone throughout the country. Each member of the surveillance team must be in possession of a mobile phone. Operators often find themselves out of radio range and the only means of communication is the mobile telephone.

> Be cautious when using mobile telephones and video cameras at the same time.The transmissions from the phone interfere with the video picture and can cause extensive electronic damage to the camera.

Radios

Communications are a very important factor in surveillance work where investigators have to work as a team. Therefore radio equipment is esential and has to be:

- Reliable and robust
- Have sufficient transmiting/receiving range
- Portable
- Secure
- Simple to operate

Radios come in various forms, the main two types being hand held transceivers, (the walkie-talkie) or vehicle mounted sets. Both sets have their advantages and disadvantages:

Vehicle Mounted Sets

Vehicle mounted sets (as their name suggests) are normally mounted and concealed in a surveillance vehicle and will give you a high transmitting range, drawing their power from the vehicles battery. An output of 5 watts or more with an external magnetic mounted antenna (mag mount) will provide a range of over seven miles.

It will not be practical to have a mag mount antenna located in the centre of your car roof as it would look conspicuous. Therefore locate it on the rear bumper or inside the car itself. A purpose built antenna fitted into the roof or wing of the car, made to look like an ordinary radio aerial is much preferred and more covert.

A vehicle mounted set requires 12 volts DC to operate and can also be used in a static O.P. when greater transmission distances are required. The radio set can draw its power from a car battery or a regulated mains power supply down to 12-13volts.

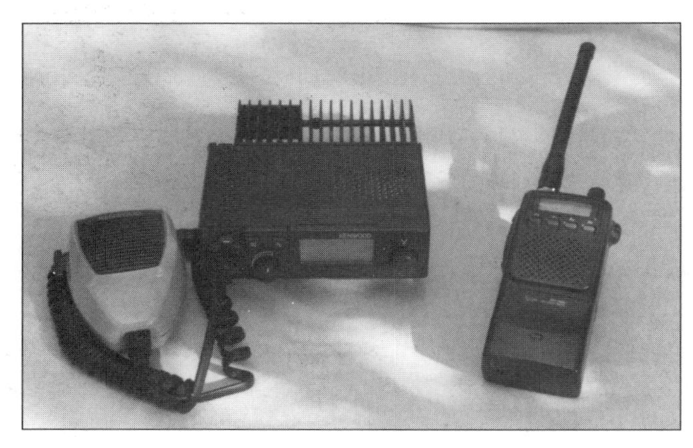

VHF Car Set and Hand Set.

Hand Held Sets

Radio hand sets offer more flexibility, they can be carried about your person during foot surveillance, located in your car or used in a rural O.P. as they have their own power supply. They can be fitted with accessories that will enable you to use the radio covertly, such as an ear piece and concealed microphone, and they also utilise their own short antenna.

When used in a vehicle, the transmission range can be greatly increased by connecting the hand set to a mag mount or a purpose fitted antenna as described above.

Should you have to operate a hand held set whilst in the street or out in the open with no ancillaries, hold the set upside down so that the antenna is not visible. It would then appear that you are talking on a mobile phone.

Covert Radio Systems

The more professional accessories comprise of a carry harness similar to that of a pistol shoulder holster which carries the radio. Built into the harness is the antenna, microphone and an induction device which 'transmits' voice to a small ear piece placed in the ear. There are no tell tale wires to the ear piece which appears very similar to a hearing aid.

Covert radio harness worn by a female operator.

For women operators, the set can either be body worn or concealed in a handbag. In this instance the microphone, inductor and PTT switch are all contained within the shoulder strap. These handbags are in common use by store detectives.

A covert system is a must for any foot surveillance work. Most professional surveillance operators carry a handheld set in a covert fashion in addition to their main car sets. Using the covert system was once described as 'the nearest you would ever get, to being telepathic'.

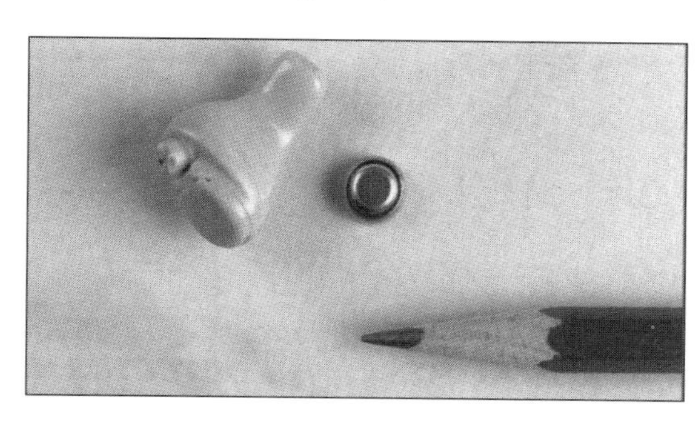

Covert, wireless earpiece.

Frequencies

Two different wave lengths are available to the commercial investigator and the correct one should be selected to obtain maximum performance for the type of area that you are normally working in.

- UHV or Ultra High Frequency should be used in very built up areas or if you are constantly working in buildings.

- VHF or Very High Frequency is the most commonly used and is ideal for most situations, it is adequate for both built up areas and out in the open.

It is preferable to have a power output of at least 5 Watts to provide you with sufficient transmitting range.

If you purchase your own VHF/UHF sets, an operators licence has to be obtained from the Department of Trade. This is usually organised by the radio dealer, the licence costs approximately £140.00 per year and can cover up to 10 radio sets. When the licence is issued you receive an operating frequency onto which the radios are set. In the VHF range, the frequency is normally between approximately 163 - 175 MHz.

Due to over crowding of the airwaves within this frequency range, it is possible that you will hear other people on the air who are using the same frequency and likewise, they would be able to hear you. This 'sharing' of frequencies could create a problem during surveillance as your commentary would be interrupted and third parties will be able to hear your commentary.

Many modern radio systems utilise a system called CTCSS coding. This system enables the radio set to automatically transmit a coded signal to your other sets and 'opens them up' to receive your messages only.

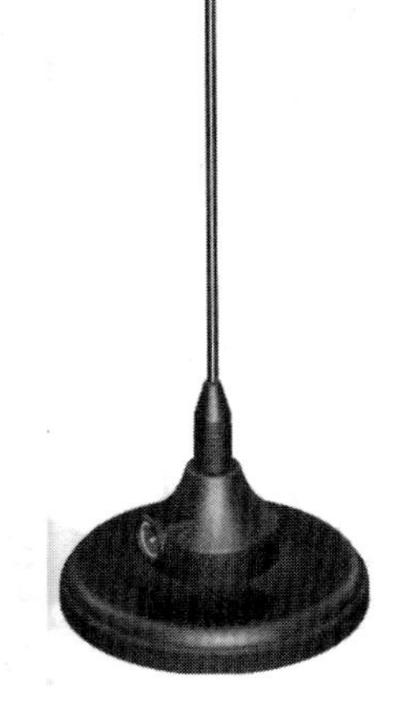

Magnetic mount aerial.

Radios using the same frequency without the compatible CTCSS coding will not be able to break in to your commentary nor will you be able to receive their transmissions.

Radios that transmit encrypted, (or scrambled), signals are available to the investigator and are essential if you are sending very sensitive information.

Care of Your Radios

There are a few rules which ensure that you get the most out of your radio equipment which is essential as they can be costly to replace:

- Always keep them clean and dry.
- Never switch the set on unless there is an antenna fitted, you will damage the set.
- Fully discharge the battery before recharging.
- Turn the set off when changing batteries.
- Be careful when removing ancillaries, you may damage connections and sockets.

The induction loop and microphone worn around the operator's neck.

Radio Callsigns

The Police, Military and other agencies use specialist call signs as a matter of course. Call signs not only identify the individual operator but also give an indication to what unit, sub-unit or team he belongs to. Complex callsigns and networks are only necessary when there are many operators on the ground with varying tasks. In the surveillance role we tend to keep to a personal callsign, i.e. Peter (PAPA), Robert (ROMEO) etc.

Establishing Communications

Prior to commencement of the task, make sure that all radios are working properly and carry out a radio check to ensure that every one can transmit and receive each other. If there is a problem, sort it out there and then before embarking on the task. Ensure that the batteries are charged and that antennas are fitted correctly. Fresh batteries should be placed in covert earpieces, ready for use.

When calling a station always state the other persons call sign first and then state your own. So that PAPA wanting to speak to ROMEO would be:

Voice Procedure	Meaning
"ROMEO, PAPA"	**(Romeo this is Papa)**
"ROMEO, send"	**(This is Romeo, send your message)**

Radio Check!

The sequence of a radio check between callsigns PAPA and ROMEO (with PAPA sending), would be:

"ROMEO, PAPA, radio check"

"PAPA, okay over" (*'difficult'* if barely audible, or *'unworkable'* if message is not understandable)

"ROMEO, okay out"

If you do not get a reply, send another Radio Check. If this still does not get a reply send over the air "Nothing Heard Out".

If the other station is able to hear you they will know that you are unable to receive them. In addition any other team members will know then that there is a communication problem and would then be able to offer to relay any messages.

Many people from various organisations use the voice procedure that is best suited to them. In surveillance, the radio commentary has to be fast, accurate and to the point, to this end it is greatly abbreviated and pro-words such as OVER, OUT and RECEIVED are dropped altogether.

Rather than use a 'mag mount', an antenna can be fitted to look like part of the vehicle.

Voice Procedure

There are various common phrases or words used when transmitting called 'pro-words' that are used frequently and mean the following:

Pro-word	Meaning
OVER	I have finished transmitting and wish you to answer.
OUT	End of message and transmission.
ROGER	Message received.
WAIT	Used as a temporary break in transmission, no one should interrupt.
SAY AGAIN	Repeat your last message.
RADIO CHECK	An offer to test comms which requires a reply i.e Okay.
I SPELL	Used prior to spelling out a name in Phonetic Alphabet.
NOTHING HEARD	When no acknowledgement is received when calling another station, the phrase "Nothing Heard - Out!" is used. This lets the recipient know that you cannot hear him even when he may be able to hear you.
RELAY TO.	Used when asking to relay, (or pass on) a message to a station that is having difficulty receiving the calling station.
PERMISSION	When operating in a large team and a member wishes to say something, he should call the team leader or eyeball and ask for PERMISSION to speak. This avoids the interruption of important commentary.
STANDBY!	Used to put the team on alert. This is never to be used in replace of 'WAIT'.

At the rear of the book there is a Glossary of Terms which details further pro-words and phrases commonly used in surveillance voice procedure.

Phonetic Alphabet

When words or car registrations have to be spelt out over the air the 'Phonetic Alphabet' is often used and is internationally recognised as a means of doing so. This is so that the letters of the words cannot be mistaken for any other and thus avoid confusion.

A	ALPHA	N	NOVEMBER
B	BRAVO	O	OSCAR
C	CHARLIE	P	PAPA
D	DELTA	Q	QUEBEC
E	ECHO	R	ROMEO
F	FOXTROT	S	SIERRA
G	GOLF	T	TANGO
H	HOTEL	U	UNIFORM
I	INDIA	V	VICTOR
J	JULIET	W	WHISKY
K	KILO	X	X RAY
L	LIMA	Y	YANKEE
M	MIKE	Z	ZULU

COMMENTRY DURING A MOBILE SURVEILANCE

During a mobile surveillance, a running commentary should be given by the lead vehicle (eyeball) to the remainder of the team to inform them of the Subjects movements and intentions. Commentary during a mobile surveillance is described fully in the relevant chapter on mobile surveillance.

Radio commentary has to be quick, precise and easily understandable.

RADIO SECURITY

Radio transmissions are open to interception and so security is an important factor when transmitting a message. There is little you can do to avoid interception, except use 'secure' radios which encrypt all messages. These are available to surveillance operators but can be very costly.

In order to minimise the risk of interception the following should be considered:-

- Use mobile telephones to send sensitive information.
- Keep transmissions to a bare minimum.
- Change frequency regularly.
- Refrain from sending 'identifiers' such as street names, place names etc.
- Use pre-arranged code words and phrases.
- Use Spot codes.

SPOT CODES

Spot codes are used to designate road names and junctions by means of allocating them a colour and a number. This provides two things, security on the net, (by not having to give specific road names over the air), and also to quickly communicate to the rest of the team, the targets location and intentions, and even team members locations.

Spotting easily identifies locations, keeps radio transmissions to a minimum and keeps them secure.

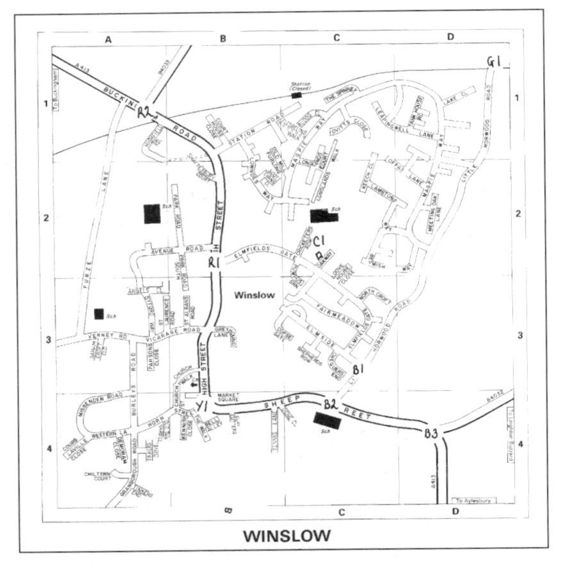

WINSLOW

Just by stating, "Subjects Blue One to Red One", tells a picture of what direction the Subject is travelling in and also his approximate location. When a team is deployed on the ground a mobile operator will be assigned an area to 'plot up' on and cover an area such as the Blues, Reds, or Greens etc.

Depending on the locality, a small number of streets in the vicinity can be spotted, alternately a small village could have all its major junctions spotted, as shown in the colour diagrams.

HAND SIGNALS

Hand signals are to be used when there is no other means of communication or when silence has to be maintained in a situation such as a rural O.P.

IDENTITIY CODES

As previously mentioned, the security of information given out over a radio is paramount. Without encrypted radios it would not be practical to give sensitive information such as names, addresses, telephone numbers and vehicle details over the air. Anyone being able to monitor your frequency and channel will soon know about the Subject of your enquiry.

In addition, unidentified people or premises should be given an identity if they cannot be named. It is possible that the Subject of a surveillance will meet up with others who are unknown to you and they will require to be identified or given a name.

There is a simple system which lets us assign identifier codes to our Subject and anyone he/she has contact with.

For example:-

- A **male** is referred to as an **ALPHA**
- A **vehicle** is referred to as a **BRAVO**
- A **property**, such as a house or building, is a **CHARLIE**
- A **female** is referred to as an **ECHO**

INDIVIDUALS

When used in context, the primary Subject, (if it is a male), would be known as **'Alpha 1'**. Should he meet up with another male, that male would then become **'Alpha 2'** and so on.

In a similar fashion, the primary female Subject would be known as **'Echo 1'.** Or if 'Alpha 1' is your Subject, his wife or partner may be assigned as '**Echo 1'.**

By assigning individuals I.D. codes it creates less confusion when giving a radio commentary. During a surveillance, the Subject may meet up with an unknown male (who could be described as male, white, thick black hair wearing a blue jumper with a white stripe across). Rather than use this awkward description every time you want to mention him, it is easier to refer to him as **'Alpha 2'.**

VEHICLES

The primary vehicle used by 'Alpha 1' would be **'Bravo 1'**. Should you arrive at 'Alpha 1's home address to commence a surveillance and find two vehicles in the driveway they could be designated '**Bravo 1'** and **'Bravo 2'**. Any subsequent vehicle related to the task would be further assigned '**Bravos 3, 4, 5**' etc.

PREMISES

In a similar fashion any property or building is referred to as a **'Charlie'.** The primary building such as 'Alpha 1's home address would be referred to as '**Charlie 1',** his place of work as '**Charlie 2**' and so on.

Procedure

Radio commentary has to be clear, concise and quick. The terms listed above assist in the speed of transmissions, making them understandable by all. For example, the following message given by a 'trigger' is long winded and insecure:-

> **"STANDBY STANDBY, That's Mr. Jones and his wife leaving the house, walking past the blue Escort and getting into the red Peugeot. Wait."**

and could be given as,

> **"STANDBY STANDBY, Alpha 1, Echo 1, exit Charlie 1 going complete Bravo 2. Wait."**

or another example,

> **"That's Mr. Jones and the male with the long grey coat and beard walking from the blue Escort back into the office building".**

could be given as

> **"Alpha 1, Alpha 2, foxtrot from Bravo 1 to Charlie 2".**

You will note that the messages are shorter, to the point and to some extent, encrypted. The system is simple and effective when used properly and eliminates the need to mention any names that should otherwise be given in 'clear'.

It is the task of the team leader to designate all initial identity codes on a briefing sheet prior to any surveillance task, which each operator will be given.

Operators Brief

A1: Alan MORRIS
35yrs, 5'10"tall, athletic build, cropped fair hair.

B1: Red Ford Fiesta (A123 BCD)

B2: Dark green Vauxhall Astra (B456 EFG)

C1: 15 Church Street, Clayton, Anytown, AN1 3TL.

C2: Techno Ltd, Unit 4, Abbey House, Abbey Road, Anytown.

C3: Techno (Systems) Ltd, 44-47 High Street, Othertown.

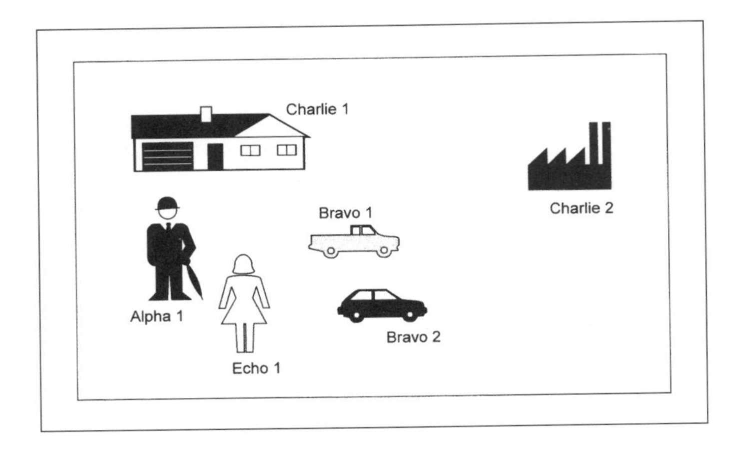

Encryption Of Numerical Information

When other sensitive information such as telephone numbers, house numbers or vehicle registrations have to be transmitted by radio they should be encrypted in the event that they are intercepted by an unauthorised listener.

A simple system we call '**LUDO**' can be used to transmit numerical figures. The pro-word 'LUDO' should always be given prior to the numbers being sent, so that the recipient knows they are encrypted.

Should you want to transmit the telephone number: **750259,** reverse the figures so that it becomes **952057.**

When you transmit your message, it would be in the form of,

"Telephone number, LUDO 952057".

The recipient having heard the pro-word LUDO, then reverses the figure to obtain the original number.

In the same manner, house numbers or vehicle registrations can be given so that **A123 ABC** becomes **LUDO A321 ABC,** etc.

There are many systems of encoding numerical information, one other simple method is to double the original number before it is transmitted. It does not matter which system you use, so long as the recipient knows what to do with the information in order to make sense of it.

> If in doubt, send sensitive information by mobile telephone.

CHAPTER FIVE

Specialist Equipment

The investigator will make use of his knowledge and experience to assess a situation and decide how best to tackle the problem to achieve a result. To do this he will have to make maximum use of what equipment is available to achieve it.

The equipment he chooses has to be cost effective, long lasting, efficient and most importantly - reliable. It is not always the best policy to buy a cheap alternative if the success of the investigation depends upon it.

The list for equipment is endless, but listed below are items that are frequently used in surveillance tasks.

The minimum pieces of equipment an operator should carry on his person or in his vehicle are:-

- Radio
- Dictaphone
- Log Sheets
- Camera
- Binoculars
- Mobile Phone
- Maps
- Money

Surveillance Vans

An important piece of equipment is the surveillance van. This van can be parked and appear to be unattended but has an operator sat in the back. He is then able to observe, record and report events taking place outside. It can also be used to provide the 'trigger' to the surveillance.

The type of van is very much up to personal preference, the Ford Escort and Fiesta models are ideal. The Escort is a popular van and is roomy, the older models also have two small windows situated behind the front seats which give the ability to view or photograph when the vehicle is parked 'side on'. The Fiesta, although small, is roomy enough and comfortable and is small enough to park almost anywhere. It is not a high vehicle and will therefore not stand out in a line of traffic. From the front and rear it looks like a car and therefore can also be used for mobile surveillance. You will be required to make certain alterations to the vehicle, some of which will be essential.

Colour

Which colour should your van be? If it is white will it stand out or should it be a dark colour? The choice is yours, where dark vans will not stand out as much, a white van can be used just as well as there are many of them about.The van can be left plain or magnetic removable signs can be used to change its appearance.

Observation

Obviously you will need to be able to observe your Subject without him being able to see you. The rear windows of the van should be covered with a film that gives you the ability to look out without anyone being able to see in. Many different types are available and come in roll form from car accessory dealers.

This 'Mirror Tint' comes in colours of silver, gold and blue. When applied, visibility out is near perfect whilst from the outside it is almost impossible to see in unless pressed against the glass or in certain light conditions. Many tradesmens' vans have this film fitted and so it does not always stand out or appear odd.

Another film similar to mirror tint is the Smoke Tint. This is black in colour and is just as effective when the inside of the van is made light proof from the front. The smoke tint is more preferable as it does not tend to stand out as much as the reflective mirror. Another alternative is to have a false wall built at the rear doors through which you will be able to observe.

As mentioned, the rear of the van has to be made light proof from the front for the windows to be effective. Plywood or a curtain suspended from a rail behind the drivers seat is sufficient. This also gives you the ability to view through the front and side windows, when necessary.

Windows and Vision

Your surveillance van needs to be operational in all weathers. A rear windscreen wiper is essential in the event of rain. You should be able to operate it from within the rear and without the ignition being switched on. Likewise in cold or damp weather the inside of the window is likely to mist up, therefore the screen 'de-mister' should be rewired to enable it to be operated in the same way. If your vehicle is going to be adapted, it is recommended to use a secondary battery rather than the vehicle's primary battery so not to run the vehicle battery flat.

Interior

The insides of the van should be panelled with plywood and painted black. This provides you with insulation from the cold, makes the vehicle more sound proof and enables you to attach any fittings such as a shelf or radio etc.

Something comfortable to sit on should be provided such as a bean bag. There is nothing worse than being uncomfortable and cramped for long periods of time, always try to sit facing the Subject rather than having to crane ones neck - it becomes uncomfortable after a short period.

Some form of ventilation should be provide by means of a proper ventilator or by just opening the front windows half an inch or so. In hot weather fresh air is required, in colder weather a flow of air is required to prevent windows from misting.

It may not always be viable to observe through the rear window and so the vehicle should be parked in such a manner that viewing is done through the front windscreen or through the side windows whilst sat in the back. If the weather is extremely cold it may be wise to put some form of hot water bottle on the dashboard under a cloth to prevent the glass from misting and freezing. The rear view mirror should be detachable to enable a clear view and prevent an obstruction for taking photographs.

Alarms

In addition to a standard vehicle alarm, a second alarm horn could also be easily installed, to be operated manually from within by means of a switch. On occasions, Third Party curiosity may invite them to take a closer look at the unfamiliar vehicle nearby, a quick burst of high decibel alarm as they touch the vehicle would possibly keep them at bay! In addition it would deter car thieves from stealing the vehicle whilst you are still in the rear.

Food & Drinks

Take adequate food and drinks for the duration of your stay. Avoid messy foods and a flask is indispensable. Ensure that you take plenty of water in hot weather to avoid dehydration, some vans can soon become like baking ovens.

Hygiene Provisions

You may be in situ for many hours where it may not be possible to leave to use the toilet. Therefore adequate provision has to be made for urinating or defacating.

Keys

Once in position the keys should be removed from the ignition and placed in a handy spot by the dashboard or easy access. A member of the team should also carry a spare set to be used when the van is being inserted and extracted.

RADIO EQUIPMENT

Communications are a very important factor in surveillance work where investigators have to work as a team. Therefore the correct equipment is paramount and is discussed in detail in the separate chapter on Communications

OPTICS

As an aid to your vision and to bring your Subject 'closer', various optical instruments are available, they should be handled with care and the lenses protected at all times.

Binoculars

There are many different types available and a pair should be selected for their cost, robustness, size and magnification. It is not always the best thing to opt for the most powerful pair you can lay your hands on nor the pair that will fit into the smallest of pockets.

Magnification

The power of a pair of binoculars refers to the number of times the Subject in view is magnified. Lenses with a power of 'times 8' (8x) magnify the Subject 8 times. This has the effect of making an object which is 400 metres away appear to be only 50 metres away.

Binoculars are commonly quoted with a magnification number such as 8 X 25. As mentioned the 8x refers to the lens magnification, the 25 relates to the diameter in millimetres of the objective lens (the larger lens at the front). This is important as the larger the objective lens is, the more light will reach your eyes. If you intend to use your binoculars mostly in the dark hours such as dusk and dawn, then the larger the objective lens the better.

A magnification of about 10 times is suitable for most purposes. Any higher could result in sore eyes and headaches if used for long periods of time.

Telescopes or Spotting Scopes

Telescopes are ideal when in a static location and you require more viewing power than binoculars. The magnification/lens size guides are the same as for binoculars. However, with a more powerful scope the field of view may be quite narrow. In this case it would be useful to have it mounted on a tripod as holding the scope would not be steady.

Many telescopes utilise a zoom facility which enables you to range the power from 8x through to 25x and upwards. If using a zoom lens always focus at its closest point and then pull out of the zoom to the required setting.

Lens Hoods

When viewing a Subject always be aware of the position of the sun. If it is to your front remember that any direct sunlight entering the optics will also be magnified and may cause blindness. The light may also be reflected off the lens and be seen to glint by your Subject. To remedy this, a piece of fine dark netting, (or stocking), held over the lens with an elastic band should suffice without distorting your image. This will cut down reflection and protect your eyes. In addition a purpose made 'lens hood' will prevent stray light from reflecting off the lens.

Night Vision Optics

Night vision equipment is divided into two categories:

Passive and Active

Active devices are always operated in conjunction with an Infra Red light source. The viewing device allows observation in total darkness, without the observer being seen. On looking through the scope nothing will be seen unless there is an amount of infra red light present to illuminate the Subject. Infra red light can be provided by means of a special filter, which is placed over the front of torches, vehicle headlights and lamps etc. On viewing through the device and illuminating the area with an invisible infra red light source, the Subject can be observed clearly in the darkest of conditions.

Infra red equipment is cheaper than image intensifiers but has the disadvantage of having to use an active additional light source.

This hand held image intensifier can be fitted to most SLR or video cameras.

Passive devices are called Image Intensifiers. They do not rely on an additional light source such as infra red to provide a clear view in darkness, but rely on the available light in the sky, (which the eye cannot see in darkness), which comes from stars, moonlight and glow. The intensifier magnifies the available light by millions of times to produce an image. This image (as with Infra Red), is viewed on a screen within the device and is seen as shades of contrasting green, white and black.

Image intensifiers can also 'see' infra red light and can be used in conjunction with an infra red light source. This enables viewing in shadows and areas of low light.

Many devices are on the market, some are ex Soviet military and can be bought fairly cheaply for a couple of hundred pounds but the quality is very poor and they cannot be adapted to be used with cameras. At present there are four generations of devices. The first being rather bulky and heavy, the fourth generation being lightweight, compact and visually very clear.

Never switch on or use these devices in daylight, unless they are fitted with the correct filters as the internal components can be damaged.

Night Vision Photography
Some of the latest light intensifying scopes can be attached to SLR cameras and Camcorders using specially designed fittings. This provides very good quality, low

light photographs. High Speed film should be used to enable fast shutter speeds (the scope adds length to the lens and so creates camera shake). The camera should be operated manually and tested to check if the cameras metering system functions correctly. If not, experiment by bracketing exposures to give you the correct and best settings to use.

Image Intensifier fitted to standard SLR camera.

When fitted to video recorders, images are immediately available on the viewfinder or monitor, therefore focusing and aperture settings can be adjusted as required.

At the time of writing, the Sony Corporation have produced an 8mm video recorder (camcorder) that utilises a system called 'Nightshot'. This camera can be used in complete darkness and has its own built in infra-red lamp.

Infra Red Light Source Devices

As already mentioned infra red light from a torch fitted with a special I.R filter enhances the performance of image intensifiers. Other devices are available which can be used for covert applications such as:

- **I.R Beacon**

  This small device, the size of a match box, emits infra red light from a series of diodes. This beacon is battery powered and can last for four days, providing enough I.R light to illuminate a small sized area such as a door way or a small room. This beacon can be concealed in a target area to be viewed and then observed from a distance.

This small beacon emits invisible, infra-red light and will illuminate areas when viewed through night vision scopes. It can be used in conjunction with a 'trip wire' to illuminiate a gate being opened etc.

- **Chemical Lightsticks**

  Chemical Lightsticks, (manufactured by Cyalume), provide a disposable invisible light source. These lightsticks are in the form of a sealed plastic tube containing chemicals. When activated (by bending) they produce an intense light source, (obtainable in many different colours) and last for 8 hours. An infra red light stick, when activated, emits no light that can be seen by the eye but when viewed through I.R goggles or an image intensifier it will illuminate a small area with invisible light. These are particularly useful illuminating dark doorways or marking access routes when retrieval is not paramount. In addition they can be attached to a 'trip wire' device which will activate the lightstick when a gate is opened or someone walks across the wire etc.

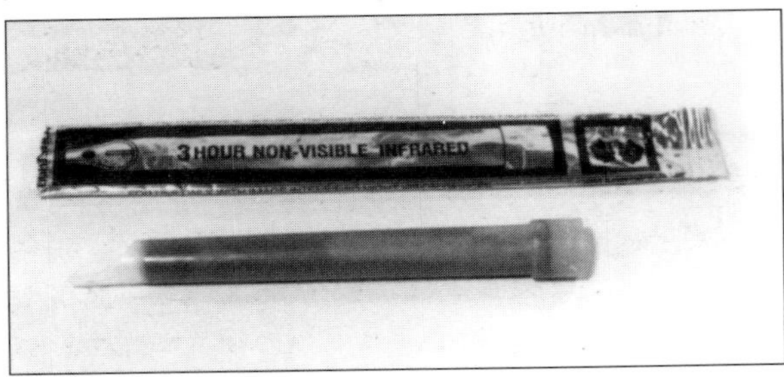

This disposable 'light stick' emits infra-red light and is used in conjunction with night vision scopes.

Dictaphones

Dictaphones or hand held cassette recorders are ideal for recording events as they happen when you do not have time to write any notes. Use a recorder whilst on a mobile surveillance to record events and details of the route that is being taken.

Locating Transmitters

These devices are useful when carrying out a mobile surveillance and the risk of loosing the Subject is high or the Subject is surveillance conscious. The transmitter can be attached to the Subjects vehicle or placed in goods that are likely to be moved. These devices comprise of a radio transmitter, which emits a signal, and is then picked up by a receiver. You will be able to establish the direction of the transmitter and be able to tell the distance that you are away from it. These devices require practise to use them effectively and should not be used as a substitute for real time surveillance.

Global Positioning Systems (GPS)

An alternative vehicle tracking and location system is provided by means of a GPS receiver interfaced with a GSM cellular phone. This device, (about the size of a paperback book), receives data from navigation satellites and is able to plot its position on the ground, anywhere in the world.

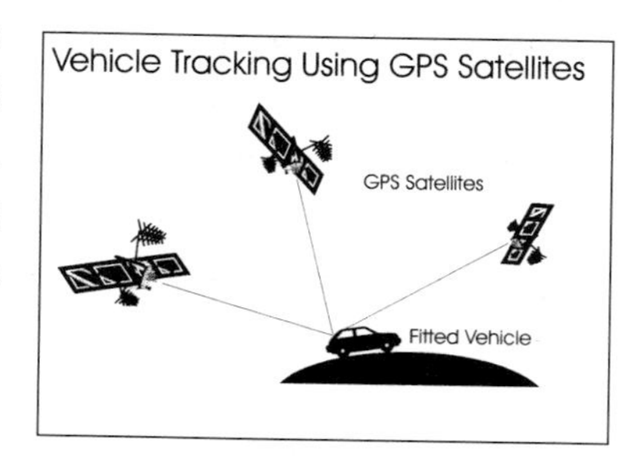

Concealed in a vehicle or vessel, this device can be interrogated by telephone, mobile phone or lap top computer. You will be able to locate the device (vehicle/vessel) by means of an Ordnance Survey grid reference, latitude/longitude reference or by digital mapping on computer. The device can be tracked anywhere in the world and can be accurate to 10 square metres on the ground. The device is an invaluable tool when tracking vehicles covertly, especially over a long term period or when the Subject is very surveillance conscious. There are a number of suppliers in the United Kingdom whose details are listed at the back of the book.

Technical Triggers

When it is not possible to observe and trigger a Subject (for one of many reasons) it would be advantageous to have a system that gives prior warning of the vehicle going mobile. The surveillance team could then be put on 'Standby' and be observing their 'areas' in order to pick up the vehicle for a follow.

A technical trigger is an electronic device which is covertly attached to the underside of a vehicle by magnets or can be wired into the vehicle itself. The device remains dormant until the vibration of the starting engine activates a transmitter. The transmitted signal is received on a unit (held by an operator) which gives a beeping tone when activated. The operator can then put the surveillance team on 'standby' and await the Subject going 'mobile'.

> The equipment list for an operator is virtually endless, as there is so much that can be used to assist in an investigation. You should remember that the equipment is only to be used as an aid and will not carry out the investigation for you. To this end the equipment is only as good as the person operating it. You should be familiar with the equipment, know how to use it proficiently in the daylight as well as in darkness and know its full limitations.

TECHNICAL SURVEILLANCE

Technical surveillance is a means where we rely on electronic surveillance devices (commonly referred to as Bugs) to gather the information for us. Should the device be installed in the best possible place, its use can be used to maximum effect.

Technical surveillance methods and types of equipment are constantly changing due to technological advancement. The methods and devices we mention in this chapter are kept to a minimum and describe basic systems only.

Technical Surveillance can fall into the following categories:-

- **Room Audio**
- **Telephone Audio**

Room Audio

Conversations taking place in a room or specific area can be listened to by the following methods.

- **Hard Wired Systems**
- **Transmitted Radio Signals**

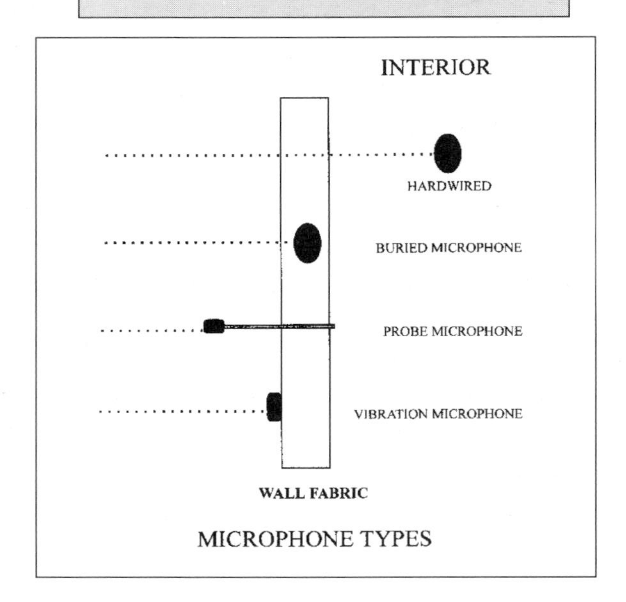

MICROPHONE TYPES

• Hard Wired Systems

A microphone placed in the target area can be concealed almost anywhere. A cable must be run from the microphone to an amplifier which gives the signal clarity especially over long distances. Head phones or a tape recorder can then be connected to the amplifier in order to monitor the conversation.

Obviously concealment of the cable is the most important factor when using this method. Redundant cables that are already in situ (such as unused telephone/computer cables or mains wiring) that are often found in offices can be used to carry the signals from the microphone to the amplifier.

This listening device is installed into the workings of a 2-way mains plug socket.

• Mains Carrier Systems

This system is very similar to a domestic 'Baby Alarm' whereby a listening unit is plugged into the mains socket of the baby's room. In another part of the house a similar receiving unit is also plugged into the wall and you can hear the sounds of the baby crying etc.

The audio is not transmitted through 'the air' but the signal is 'carried' along the mains wiring system in the house. Eavesdropping devices can be covertly installed in the mains system to operate in a similar fashion.

• Transmitted Radio Signals

Transmitters (Bugs) are small devices which can be left concealed in the target area. They will pick up conversations via a microphone and then transmit the signal to a receiving unit located nearby. This receiver in turn will be connected to a tape recorder or headphones.

Transmitters can be manufactured and supplied as 'stand alone' units or disguised as everyday objects such as calculators, pens, mains power sockets or built into briefcases etc.

Transmitters require an electrical supply in order for them to operate. They can be **Battery Operated, Mains Operated, Solar Powered** or a combination of all three.

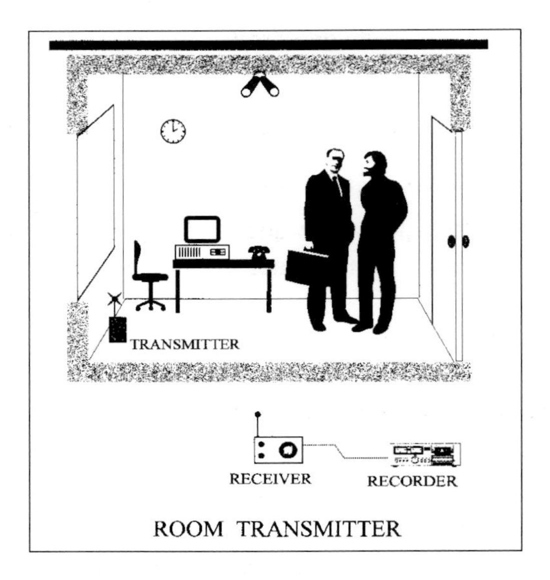

ROOM TRANSMITTER

- **Battery Operated**

  Battery operated devices are very easily installed and can operate for a number of days without having to change the batteries. Battery operated devices should only be used for short term operations otherwise you may risk compromise every time you change the batteries.

- **Mains Powered**

  Mains powered devices will be more difficult to install and you may have to isolate the power supply to avoid electric shock. Once installed, these devices will operate indefinitely so long as there is a power supply. Some mains powered devices may have a battery connected to them to act as a back up in the event of mains failure.

- **Solar Powered**

  Some devices rely on solar power to operate such as a calculator transmitter. The transmitting range of solar powered devices will not be very far.

Telephone Audio

Intercepting telephone conversations is probably the best way of technically gathering information and can be gathered in the following manner.

- **Hard Wired Telephone Tap**
- **Transmitted Signals**
- **Induction Telephone Tap**

- **Hard Wired Telephone Tap**

  A tape recorder can be connected by various means to the telephone system and can intercept conversations taking place over one particular target telephone or from any other telephone extension that is currently being used on the same circuit.

  The recorder has to be physically connected to the telephone line and the signals pass through an interfacing switching device which stops and starts the recorder as the telephone handset is lifted. These switches can operate by 'voice activation' (VOX) or by voltage 'relay' switches.

  This system is very effective and the recorder can be located in another part of the building some distance away from the target telephone.

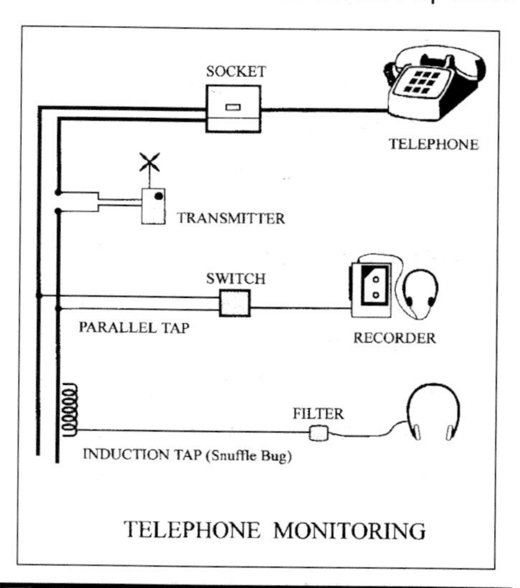

TELEPHONE MONITORING

- **Transmitted Signals**

  In a manner similar to that of room transmitters, telephone transmitting devices can send conversation over the air to a nearby receiver. The transmitters have to be connected to the line, (by splicing) at a point between the telegraph pole and the target telephone or inside the telephone itself.

Depending on how and where the device is actually installed, will reflect on whether one telephone or any other extensions will be intercepted. There are various telephone devices available, the more common types rely on the telephone line voltage to operate them. Some have a rechargeable battery built into them to provide extra transmitting power. Telephone transmitters can be supplied as 'stand alone' units or come ready made built into telephone sockets and adapters.

- **Induction Telephone Tap**

  This device, often referred to as a 'Snuffle Bug' can be used in conjunction with a transmitter or a hard wired system. The telephone line does not have to be 'broken into' and the device is difficult to detect. The device is placed on the outside of the telephone wiring and picks up signals by 'induction'. Every wire that has a current running through it radiates a magnetic field and this device is able to read the signals carried along this magnetic field.

Recorders

Conversations, whether they are room audio or telephone are more likely to be recorded so they can be listened to at a later time. There are many different types of tape recorders available some of which can record for four hours or more on a single side of a cassette.

EQUIPMENT SUPPLIERS

If you decide to purchase electronic surveillance equipment, then do so with caution. Otherwise you may find yourself with an item of equipment that is totally unsuitable to the task that you need it for. If at all possible, seek the advice of someone who has used the equipment in the past and can recommend what to use. Many suppliers buy and sell equipment, but rarely have had to use or install it whilst actually 'out in the field'. A demonstration that may sound good in an office or showroom may not necessarily be the case when installed for its designated purpose.

There are many suppliers in the United Kingdom who sell a vast range of devices and their promotional literature can often be misleading. Do not necessarily buy equipment from the company that provides an impressive glossy brochure and is likely to be London-based. You will possibly find yourself paying for the company's advertising literature and shop rent, rather than a quality item of equipment.

It is recommended that you shop around and obtain several brochures. On looking through them you will often find the same items of equipment for sale but at a vast difference in price. As an example, a crystal controlled telephone transmitter and dedicated receiver in UHF band will cost in the region of £900 from a major London supplier. Whereas from a supplier in Leeds, the same item of equipment will cost approximately £450.

When choosing a supplier, ensure that the device that you require is suitable for your requirements.

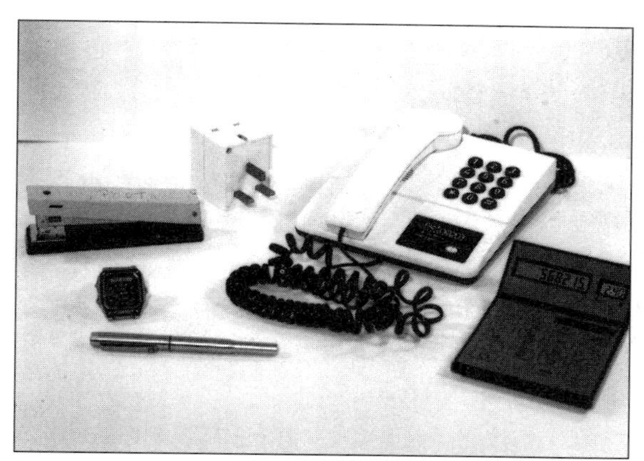

Transmitters can be concealed in many everyday objects.

- **Cassette Tape Length (recording time)**

  If choosing a tape recorder, ensure that the amount of time that you are able to record is sufficient without having to attend to the recorder. A recorder 8 Hours recording time' may mean that you will get 4 hours recording on one side of the tape, which means that you will have to physically turn the cassette over, (unless it is an auto-reverse model).

- **Transmitting Ranges**

  The majority of popular transmitters currently on the market will not operate over a distance of 200-300 metres unless used with a 'repeater'. The transmitting range of a device is dependent on so many factors that an accurate transmission distance cannot be given. Do not expect to receive signals from a device one mile away that only operates on a battery the size of a pea.

- **Battery Life**

  Remember that if you use a battery-operated transmitter, you will probably have to service it before the batteries go flat, especially in a long-term situation. To do this you may run the risk of being compromised, so ensure you know the 'actual' battery life span of the device and put it through a full test. Alternatively, find out if it can be used in conjunction with a 'long life' power pack.

- **Audio Clarity**

  It is suggested that you use only 'Crystal Controlled' transmitting devices for professional purposes. Although they are more expensive than their 'Free Oscillating' counterparts, you will find that the audio quality is much clearer. In addition, they are more suitable when using voice activated recording systems, as the signal does not fluctuate and cause interference, which can accidentally start a recorder and thus waste valuable recording tape.

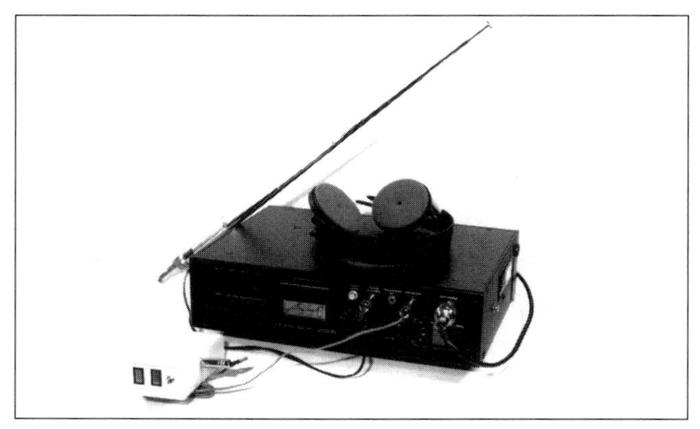

The Scanlock 2000 counter-measures equipment, used to search and locate transmitting devices.

CHAPTER SIX

Evidence & Law

Surveillance Logs and Reports. As a member of a surveillance team, you should keep a brief log of exactly what occurs and what action is taken. The team leader may keep a more detailed log of team events, (Master Log). It is important that all team members synchronise their watches and timers on photographic equipment so that the surveillance logs coincide with each other and there are no discrepancies. Remember, all oddities may be brought to the attention of a court and could quite possibly discredit your evidence.

Should you be in a static observation position, you may be able to write down a fair amount of detail about the target area and the events taking place.

Depending on the nature of the enquiry, it will effect how you log and produce your written reports. It is recommended to have the surveillance logs typed up and submitted with accompanying photographs or video tape. Reports in this format include all details and log events in a **chronological order.**

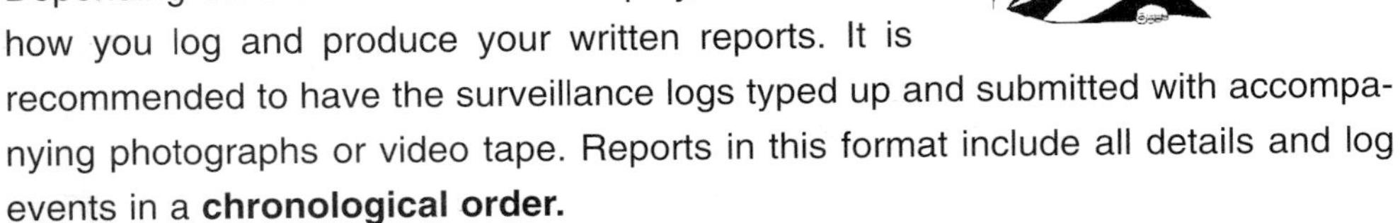

Surveillance Logs

All timings, incidents and information should be recorded in a chronological order and preferably written down in note form. The notes that you make will be regarded as contemporaneous and will possibly be used as evidence and therefore would have to be produced in court. Your notes may be written on anything at the time of the incident, (pocket book, log sheets or even the back of a cigarette packet), but once written they should be preserved as evidence, more importantly so if you are investigating a criminal activity.

It is not always necessary to use prepared log sheets but they are simple, easy to read and make life easier when they have to be typed. An example of a Log Sheet is found below. It is not always practical to hand write a log, and so a running commentary, or details of an event may have to be kept on dictaphone tape. The details on the tape should be written up as soon as practically possible. On occasions, (such as Criminal Investigations) the dictaphone tape will also have to be retained and preserved as evidence.

SURVEILLANCE LOG — **PAGE 1 of 1**
OPERATOR: *Paul King (c/s Papa)* — **DATE:** *1st Sept 97*

No.	Time	Event	Comments	Pic
1.	06.44	Team at 12 Smith St., Anytown. All curtains are closed. Parked in the drive is a red Ford Escort - Reg: K123 ABC Observations maintained	Weather clear & sunny. Call signs: Papa Golf, Kilo.	
2.	07.15	Upper curtains opened by female (slim build, short, blond hair, 35 yrs).	Wife?	
3.	07.53	Male, presumed to be Subject exits house, into red Escort (para 1) & mobile. Desc, 5'9", slim, short dark hair, dark suit, steel rimmed specs, 37 yrs.	Photos c/s Papa	1 - 4
4.	08.25	Stops at Weld Test Engineering, Globe St, Halifax & enters carrying briefcase. Parks in Visitors car park.	Photos c/s Golf	1 - 3
5.		Route: Smith St. L on North St. L on Royale St. R on A629, L on Church Road, R on Globe Road.		
6.	09.34	Subject exits above & mobile.		
7.	09.56	Stops at Raleigh Engineering, on Weeland Rd, Enters factory with briefcase.	Photos c/s Papa	5 - 7
8.	11.01	etc.		

Example Surveillance Log

Eye Witness Testimony as Evidence

If you find yourself in court giving evidence, it is possible that the Defence barrister (or opposition) will attempt to discredit your evidence or put your 'witness testimony' to some doubt in order to confuse a jury. In a famous case **(Regina -v- Turnbull 1976),** certain witnesses to an armed robbery were called to give evidence at the robbers trial, Turnbull was the getaway driver in the robbery.

These witnesses saw the robbery take place but their testimony was put to question by the Defence. Many questions were asked: *"How far away from the Defendant were you when you saw him? If you were across the street was the road busy at that time of the day? Could passing buses obscure your view? How long did you have him in sight for? Are your sure it was him? How can you be certain?"* etc.etc.

In summing up, the judge informed that jury that there should be a special need for caution when considering eye witness evidence and said that a single witness can make mistakes, several witnesses are likely to paint a more realistic picture of events but they can also still be mistaken.

This case set a precedent and barristers now use this case as a guide when cross examining eye witnesses.

> *During surveillance training courses, we show a video film of a robbery taking place to the students, after which, they are questioned about what they saw. The recurring mistakes are notable; different descriptions of the same person, a different sequence of events etc.*

If we take the case of R -v- Turnbull, and can give answers to the following points raised, we can be confident in our evidence. Using the pneumonic ADVOKATE we remember the points about which to provide detail in our surveillance logs, which you may be questioned about in court.

ADVOKATE

A Amount of Time

How long was the Subject actually in view for?

D Distance

How far away was the Subject from you?

Were you using optics such as binoculars or telephoto lenses?

Was the Subject so close that you had to avert you eyes?

V Visibility

What was the weather like? Was it foggy? Was the sun in your eyes?

Were you having to look in your rear view mirror, was it a back to front image?

Do you wear glasses? Were you wearing them at the time?

O Obstructions

Were you looking across a busy street, heavy with passing traffic?

Were you having to peer through heavy foliage?

Was there a lot of pedestrian activity?

Did the Subject go out of sight at any time?

K Known or Seen Before

Had you seen the Subject before?

Was he known to you?

Did you have a photograph to recognise him from?

Had you carried out surveillance on him before?

A Any Reason to Remember

I had reason to remember because that day in question was my birthday.

I remember the jumper he wore because I have one exactly like it.

I remember him because he was the spitting image of (someone famous).

T Time Lapse

Could your memory fail you?

What was the time span between seeing the incident and making your notes?

What was the time span between seeing the incident and making a statement?

What was the time span between seeing the incident and the identity parade?

E Errors or Discrepancies

Is it possible.........?

Is it possible that you are mistaken?

You have stated this, another witness has stated that, could you be wrong?
I have given evidence in Court when the Defence barrister went systematically through the list above. At the time I was still a 'young investigator' and had no knowledge of R -v- Turnbull or ADVOKATE but I was able to provide the correct answers to his cross examination. This was only due to correct log keeping at the time, quick thinking and having the confidence in my own evidence.

EXERCISE

As an exercise, take a recent surveillance log that you have prepared and ask yourself whether you can answer all those questions listed above about a particular important incident.

Remember a defence barrister will want to:-

- Shorten the time span that the Subject was in your sight.
- Extend the distance between you and the Subject.
- Cloud your view.
- Prove that your view was fully or partially obstructed for a short period of time.
- Intimate a wrong identity.
- Question your judgement and memory.
- Put to you any discrepancies, such as errors in your logs etc.

PRESERVATION OF PHOTOGRAPHIC EVIDENCE

The aim of the majority of surveillance tasks is to gain photographic evidence of an event taking place or to prove that a person was in a particular location at a certain date and time.

Should these photographs be used in legal proceedings, (especially criminal), then they should be handled, preserved and exhibited as any other evidence would be.There should be a documented record of the evidence when it is transferred from one person to another for reasons of continuation.

Having taken the photographs, the film should remain in your control until the photos are handed over to a legal authority such as a solicitor or the Police, when they should be exhibited with your Statements or Surveillance Logs. Should the whereabouts of the evidence be unknown at any time, it could be used by the opposition in court to discredit that evidence, claiming that it had been tampered with and altered. The most vulnerable time when the film is out of your control is when it is being processed and it is during this process when the evidence could be altered to provide an untrue image (although unlikely). To preserve the continuance of evidence it may be wise to have your photo processor sign a declaration stating that the film was processed by him/her that it had not been altered and it was handed directly back to you.

We have used this system in the past, with the document stating:

> I, Karen Bloggs of Print It Photo Processors, Anytown, have received one roll of 24 exposure Kodak film from Mr. Paul King on 21st March 1997 at 12.00hrs.
>
> The film was developed and printed on the premises by me and has not left the premises at any time. The photographs have not been altered or interfered with so as to make them false.
>
> At 16.30hrs on 21st March 1997 I handed the processed negatives and prints over to Mr. Paul King.
>
> Signed: Dated:

This procedure may seem extreme or over the top, but if the photographs recorded a criminal event such as a theft, the defence barrister will ask you, "were the photographs and negatives ever out of your control?". "Is it possible, that they could have been tampered with?" If the answer to those questions is 'Yes', then this destroys the chain of evidence and puts doubt as to the credibility of that evidence.

In the matter of video taped evidence, your original recording should be copied to be used as a 'working' copy to make further copies or make edited versions. The original tape should be labelled, secured and retained as evidence.

Camera Data Backs and Date/Time Generators

Many investigators make use of a 'data back' fitted to their camera. This device prints the date and time onto the photograph as it is taken. From an evidential point of view the date and time printed on the photo could be questioned in court, as it is possible to set an incorrect date and time on the device. Just because the photo has 12-6-94 printed on it, it does not necessarily mean that it was taken on that date.

This does not mean that using a databack is a waste of time. Having the date/time assists in the compilation of reports and logs and provides documented corroboration. It makes the pictures look more professional and would only likely be challenged in court if there were discrepancies in other parts of that evidence.

Should you make use of a data back, ensure that the timer is synchronised to your watch or the time-piece that you refer to when writing a surveillance log. Should you realise after the pictures have been taken that the timer is not synchronised with your watch, make a note on the surveillance log to this effect.

In addition, ensure the clock on your SLR camera is synchronised with your video camera if you are using both.

CHAPTER SEVEN

Mobile Surveillance

Mobile surveillance is probably one of the most difficult types of surveillance to carry out, as there are so many factors that are against you whilst following a mobile Subject. The Subject has to be followed without detection and without losing contact with him. At the same time you have to keep a log of events and actions, communicate with the other members of the surveillance team, navigate, photograph and consider the subjects future intentions.

A mobile surveillance should not be a 'mad car chase', driving at excessive speed, screeching brakes and handbrake turns, but should be done in a calm, relaxed, professional manner and most importantly, be under control.

The Surveillance Team

We refer to a mobile surveillance being carried out by a team rather than an individual. Carrying out a surveillance by one man is asking for trouble as the risk of compromise is very high from the outset and loss of contact is inevitable. An operator on his own will soon be spotted and would therefore jeopardise any further surveillance, he may also lose the Subject at the first road junction he approaches. The success of a surveillance is dependant on how many men are used, a combination of cars and motorbikes provide an effective surveillance team.

It is appreciated in the commercial sector, that clients are very cost conscious and that a surveillance can be costly to carry out. If you have to supply a potential client with an estimate of charges it is essential that you inform them of the importance of using a minimum of two investigators to carry out a mobile surveillance, which will reflect in the costs.

The Team

Prior planning would decide on the size of the team. Factors to consider are:

- Is surveillance the answer?
- Costings per operator
- The Subjects awareness
- Area that the Subject is to be in, i.e. town centres, rural or motorway and the likely areas he may visit, you may need a motorbike or footmen etc.
- Whether a static O.P. is required to act as 'trigger'.
- Is a footman required to double up with a mobile operator?

A well rehearsed and exercised surveillance team will enable a mobile surveillance to be carried out with the minimum of effort. Members can act on their own initiative without having to be instructed by the team leader, especially when the Subject comes to a STOP and the team splits to surround him. (boxes him in).

Whenever possible make use of a static operator in a van or O.P. to give you the 'trigger'. The most likely time to loose a Subject is within minutes of his departure, especially if his departure time is unpredictable.

Type of Vehicles

An ordinary production line saloon car with a reasonable sized engine to give initial acceleration, thrust and overtaking power. Colour and appearance should be as nondescript or as commonplace as possible. A vehicle will be seen but should not be noticed, so do not try to alter its appearance, i.e. extra lamps, extra mirrors (exterior or interior) etc, they will only make it distinctive. Likewise scratches, dents, damage and malfunctioning lights will also help to identify and make the vehicle noticeable. Ensure that all the wheel trims are present and are of the same style.

Ensure that all the teams vehicles are different, it would be a waste of time having two red Ford Escorts on the same task! Do not use vehicles with personalised plates or those that will easily be remembered, i.e. having the letters ROD or SPY etc.

Crew

The vehicle crew can consist of a number of operators but remember that even two men in a vehicle, (two up), can arouse suspicions, especially when waiting for a 'trigger'. I would recommend one operator per vehicle at most times, unless an operator is required to deploy on foot at short notice.

If two persons are used, decide on the tasks of driver and footman. Their appearance should fit with the vehicle and area. The second operator during the mobile phase should sit in the rear seat behind the driver in order to remain out of view giving the appearance of being 'one up'. If necessary, he can switch to the other side temporarily to show the vehicle 'two up', in addition the second operator in the rear, can easily take covert photographs when necessary. Should you have two operators in the same vehicle, consider them being different sexes which appears more natural.

If you have to sit in your car for a period, even if it's a short halt whilst following, try and move over to the passenger seat. If the Subject, (or anyone else), sees you they would naturally presume that you are waiting for your driver to return.

Do not wear brightly coloured clothing or have anything noticeable on the dashboard that draws attention. A change of jacket or the wearing of a hat for a short period is advisable.

In rural areas which are 'wide open', you will have to hang back in your vehicle from the subject. Also, rural areas are difficult for mobile operators to lie up in.

Boxing the Subject

On arrival at the point where a surveillance is to commence, carry out a recce by driving past, (or walk past), to establish the situation and act accordingly. Position the cars where all exits and approaches can be covered or 'boxed in'. Your pre-surveillance should have already decided this but if possible carry out a further recce to allow for any unexpected changes. **Check and double check that the address that you are watching is the correct address.**

Triggering the Surveillance and Picking Up

Sometimes it is not possible to trigger the Subject vehicle when he initially goes mobile and so he has to be picked up somewhere along a route that he is known to take regularly. This 'choke point' may have to be identified by map reading or identified by previous surveillances that have been carried out.

When picking up a Subject in this instance, the cars must be distributed along the route in such positions that the crew can see the Subject as it passes but they are not themselves noticeable to the Subject.

As soon as possible after the pick-up, a team member should attempt to identify that the driver, (or passenger), is the actual Subject to be followed. This may mean overtaking the Subject to get a closer look. Do not look directly at the occupants when overtaking but glance out of the corner of your eye, better still, wait until you have passed them and view them in your mirrors.

Action on a 'STANDBY STANDBY!'

As soon as the 'trigger' gives a 'STANDBY STANDBY!', the mobile units should carry out the following:-

- Instantly acknowledge with your call sign. When the team moves, no one should be left behind.
- Turn your engine on.
- Listen very carefully to the 'triggers' radio commentary, he will be giving descriptions, vehicle details and directions.
- Move from your 'plot up' position and draw near to the spot where you intend to pick up or intercept the Subject.
- Be prepared to pick up the Subject or act as back-up.

If a STANDBY is a false alarm, the 'trigger' should give 'CANCEL STANDBY', to which the team acknowledges and returns to their plot up positions.

Lead Vehicle

The lead vehicle or 'eyeball' is always in control of the surveillance and adopts the role of team leader, although an overall leader can be in charge. It is the 'eyeball' that should give a running commentary to the remainder of the team.

The lead vehicle should be changed over frequently and this depends on how long you have been in the lead and the type of route that you have been covering. Whenever the Subject has come to a halt for some reason, (delivery/entering premises etc), the lead vehicle should be changed so that a 'fresh' vehicle can lead when the Subject goes 'mobile'.

When following along motorways let the 'change over' occur by the 'eyeball' vehicle leaving at a junction and then rejoining the carriageway, whilst the back up takes over as 'eyeball'.

As lead vehicle, always drive 'normally' and be confident. Obviously you do not want to be right behind the Subject when there is no need, but common sense prevails. If approaching an obstacle such as traffic lights, a junction or a roundabout etc. get as close as possible to avoid being held back. On approaching an obstacle never 'crawl' up behind the Subject, if you do this you will soon be spotted or have the Subjects suspicions aroused. Remember, you are a public road user going about your normal daily routine and therefore you have to act normally.

Roundabouts offer a 'natural point' to change over the lead (eyeball) vehicle.

As back up (who should be close behind the eyeball), you should be ready to take over as 'eyeball' in the event that the Subject suddenly turns or stops and so your concentration must be on the Subject's actions and think ahead.

With any Subject, always attempt to use at least one vehicle for cover, and change lead vehicles as often as possible. These change overs should be carried out at natural obstacles such as roundabouts and road junctions.

Avoid pulling into the side of the road (to let your back-up through), unless you are out of sight of the Subject, such as behind a row of parked cars etc. Never rejoin the carriageway whilst still in the Subject's mirrors, he may notice you, wait until he is out of view.

Motorbikes

A surveillance riders task is fairly specialised and requires training and experience. The rider has to be very proficient in bike handling as his task is probably one of the most dangerous on the team. A good rider will be able to act on his own initiative without having to be tasked by the team leader, he will know when to hang back or come through and take the eyeball.

The use of motorbikes provide an essential aid when carrying out mobile surveillance in heavy traffic such as busy towns and cities but they do have their limitations. In their favour they are harder to notice, they are fast with good acceleration and they can access where cars can not.

In the event of having to follow slow moving vehicles, they can easily remain out of sight but have the power to quickly move up. The rider can also position himself, in the road, stop and hold traffic back in order to let the surveillance team come through when necessary.

The disadvantage of the bike is the fact that the rider is exposed, not only to the elements but to anyone watching him. A rider sat on his bike in a built up area will soon be noted as suspicious and so the biker would normally co-locate with a car until the 'Standby'. The professional surveillance rider will have his bike and helmet fitted with appropriate radio equipment.

Three Man Team Formation

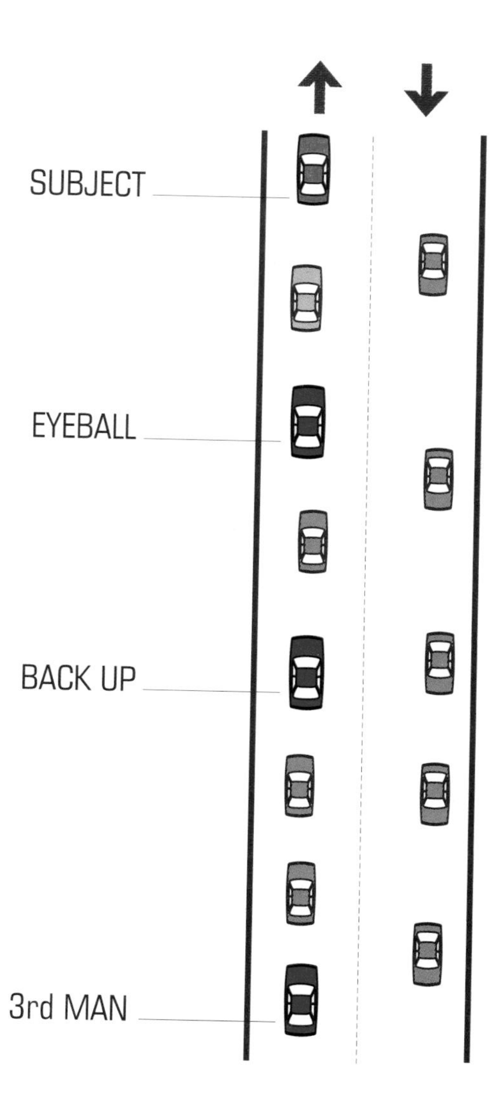

This illustration shows the subject in heavy traffic. The Eyeball has one vehicle for cover as does the Back Up behind the Eyeball. The 3rd Man remains out of sight at the rear.

Three Man Team Formation

Change of Eyeball at a Junction

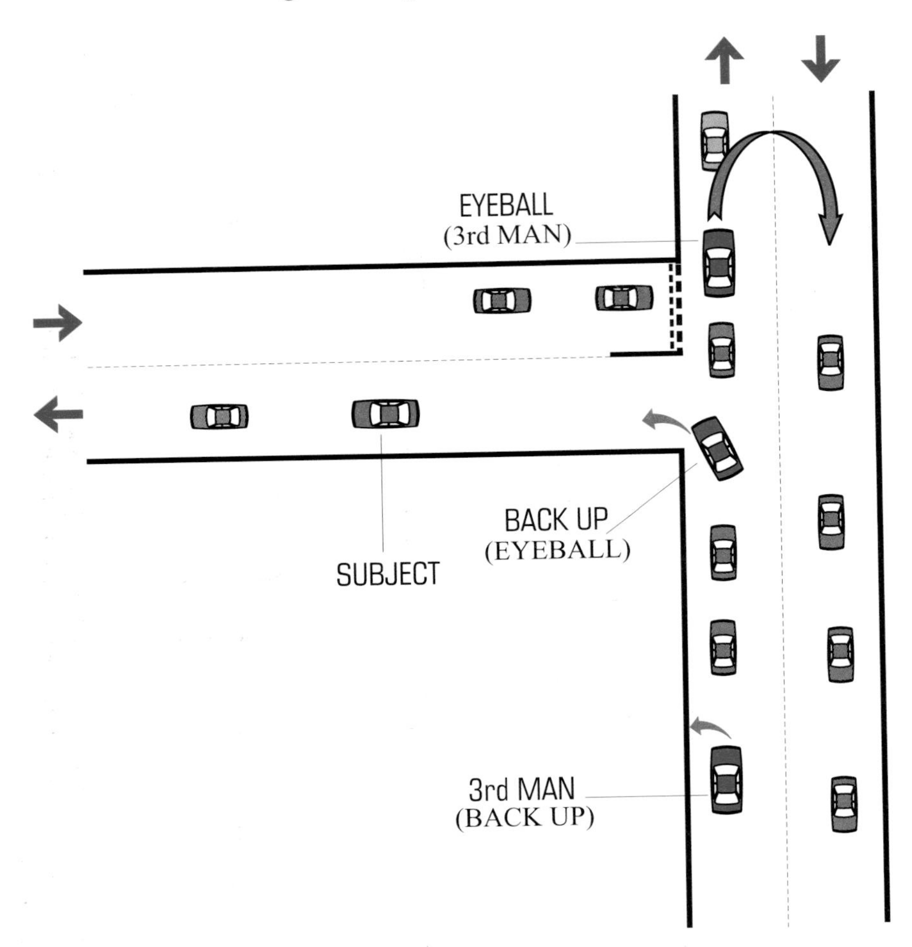

This illustration shows the subject having turned LEFT. The Eyeball has continued straight and the Back Up turns Left to take the Eyeball. The 3rd Man then becomes Back Up. The original Eyeball then manouvres to take the 3rd position.

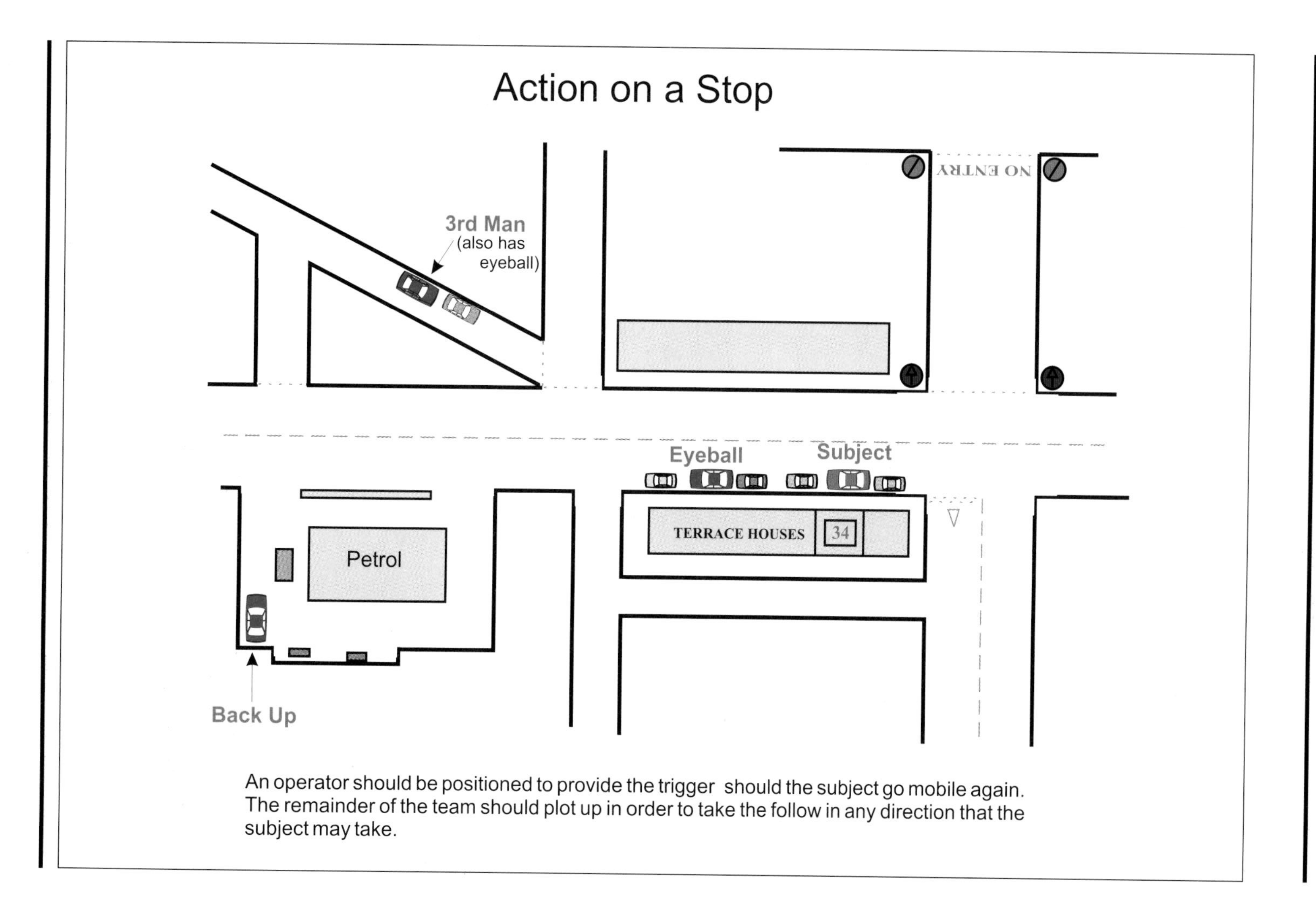

An operator should be positioned to provide the trigger should the subject go mobile again. The remainder of the team should plot up in order to take the follow in any direction that the subject may take.

Roundabout Procedure

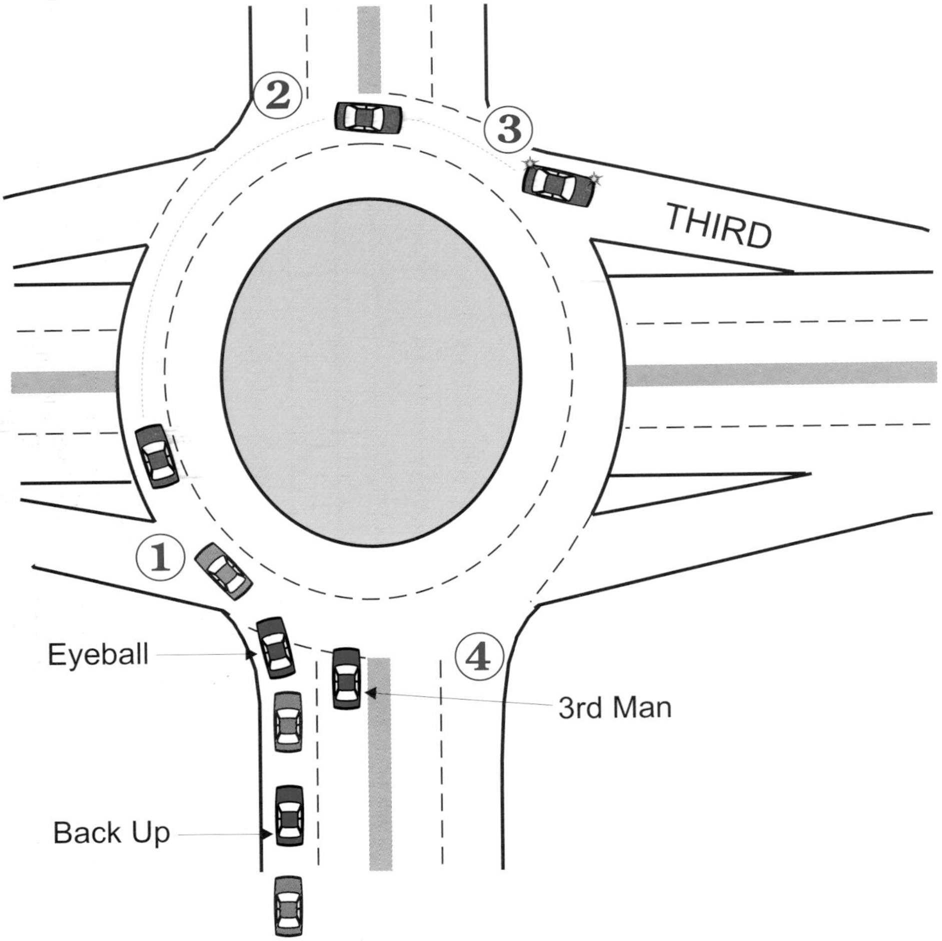

The commentary for the manouvre at this roundabout would be given as:

"NOT ONE NOT ONE, NOT TWO NOT TWO, THE THIRD THIRD AND RIGHT"

The tense changing to THIRD instead of three to indicate the exit taken.

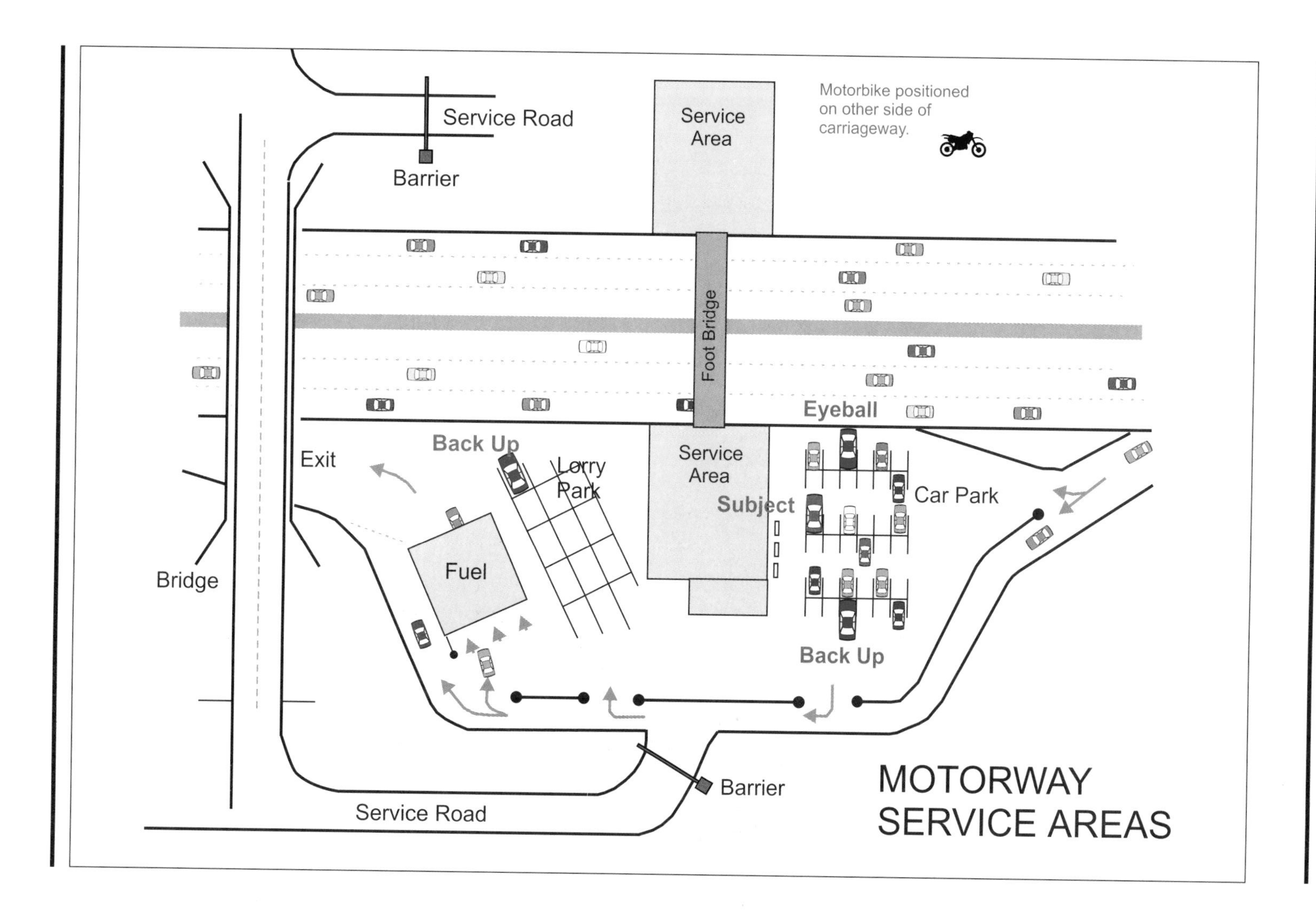

Service Road
Barrier
Service Area
Motorbike positioned on other side of carriageway.
Foot Bridge
Eyeball
Back Up
Exit
Lorry Park
Service Area
Subject
Car Park
Bridge
Fuel
Back Up
Barrier
Service Road
MOTORWAY
SERVICE AREAS

COVERT RADIO SYSTEMS

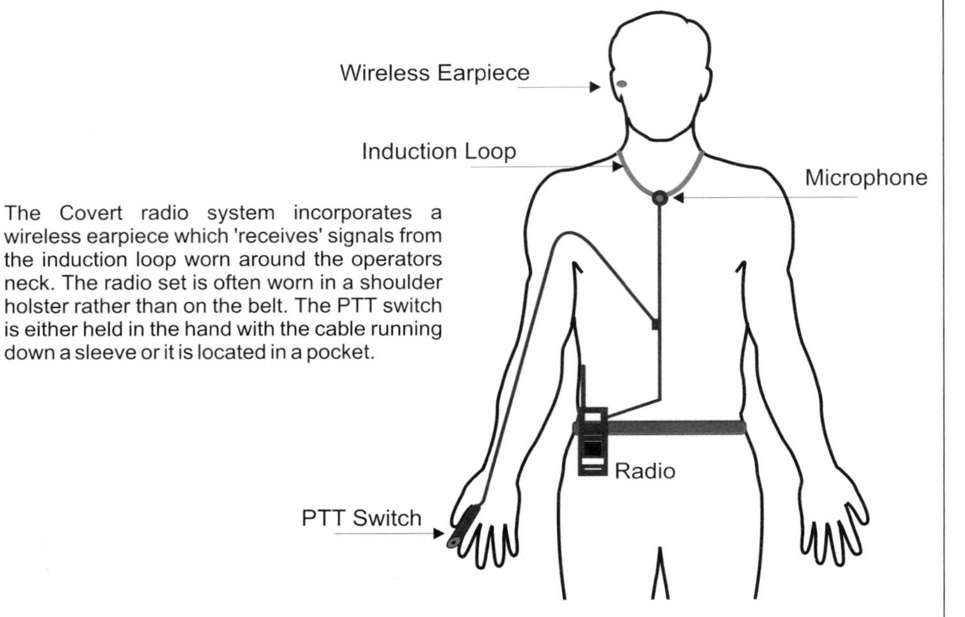

The Covert radio system incorporates a wireless earpiece which 'receives' signals from the induction loop worn around the operators neck. The radio set is often worn in a shoulder holster rather than on the belt. The PTT switch is either held in the hand with the cable running down a sleeve or it is located in a pocket.

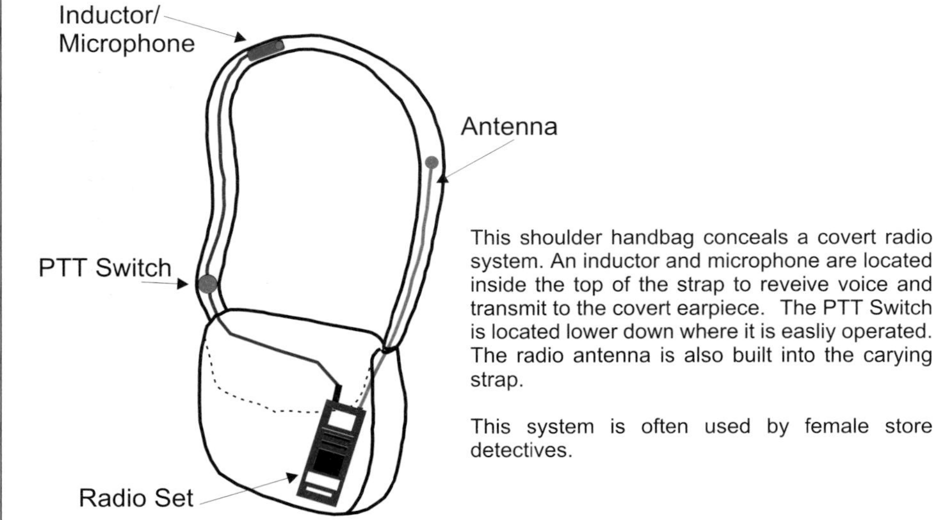

This shoulder handbag conceals a covert radio system. An inductor and microphone are located inside the top of the strap to reveive voice and transmit to the covert earpiece. The PTT Switch is located lower down where it is easliy operated. The radio antenna is also built into the carying strap.

This system is often used by female store detectives.

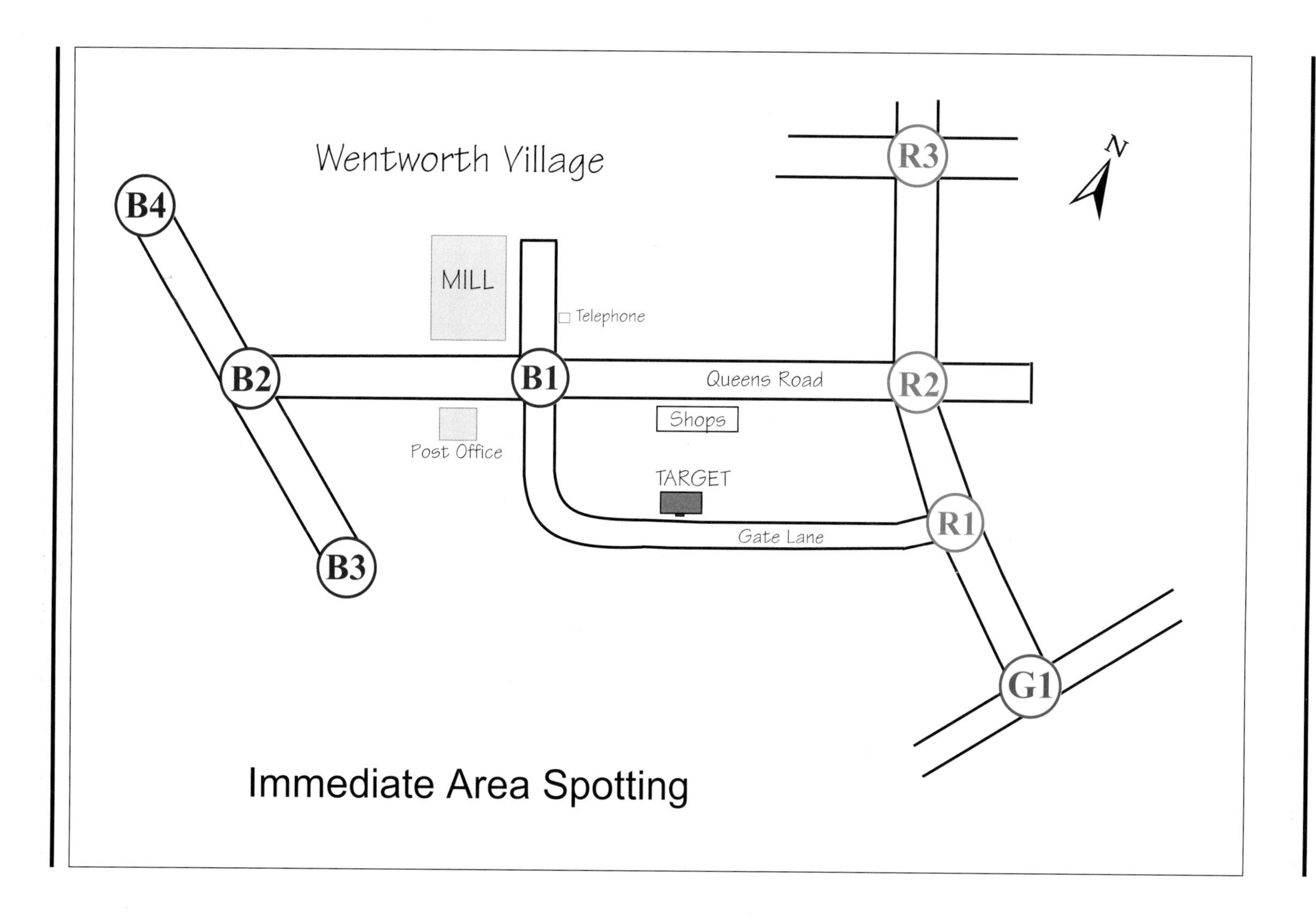
Wentworth Village
N
R3
B4
MILL
Telephone
B2
B1
Queens Road
R2
Shops
Post Office
TARGET
R1
Gate Lane
B3
G1
Immediate Area Spotting

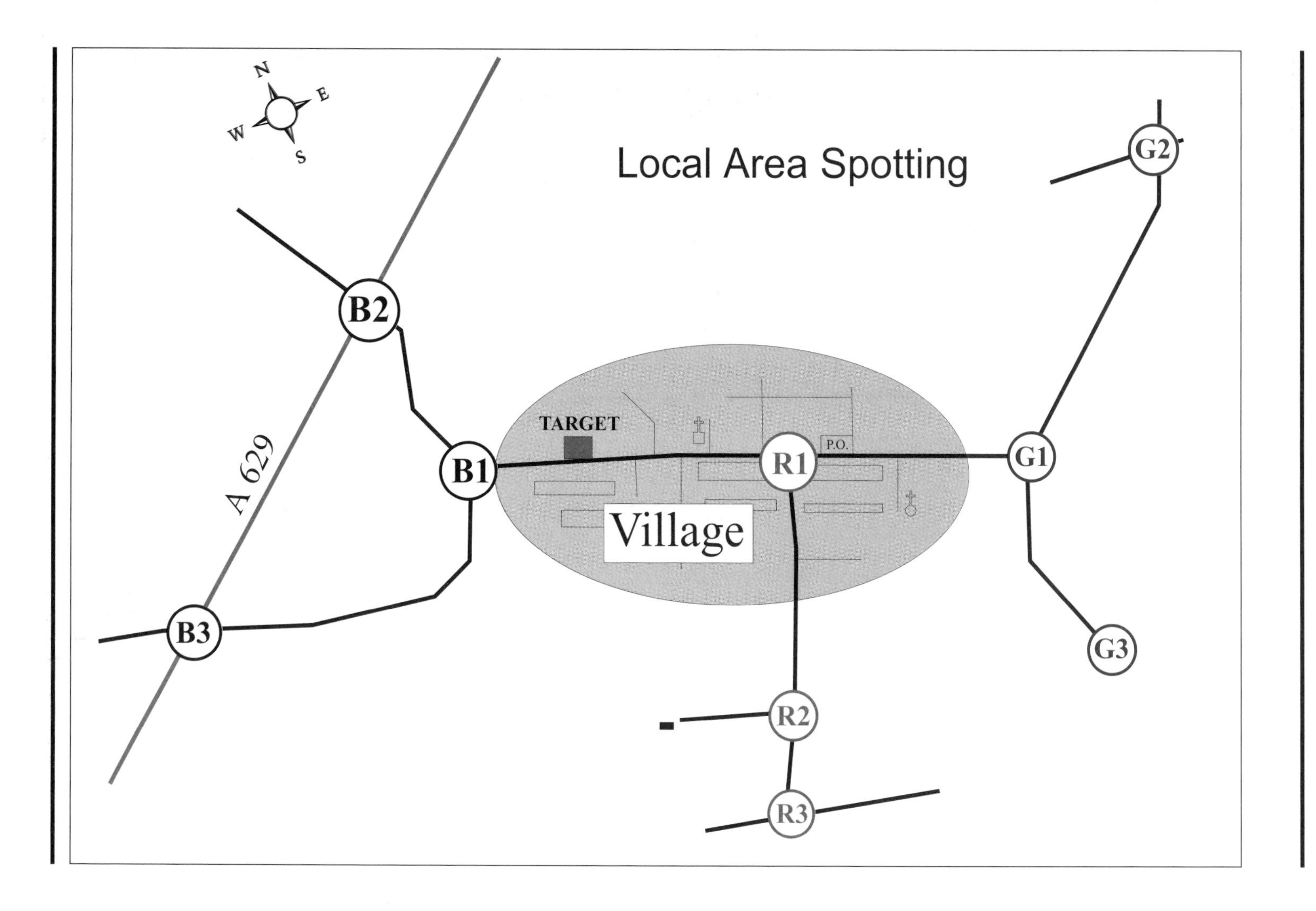
Local Area Spotting
N
E
S
W
A 629
B1
B2
B3
TARGET
P.O.
Village
R1
R2
R3
G1
G2
G3

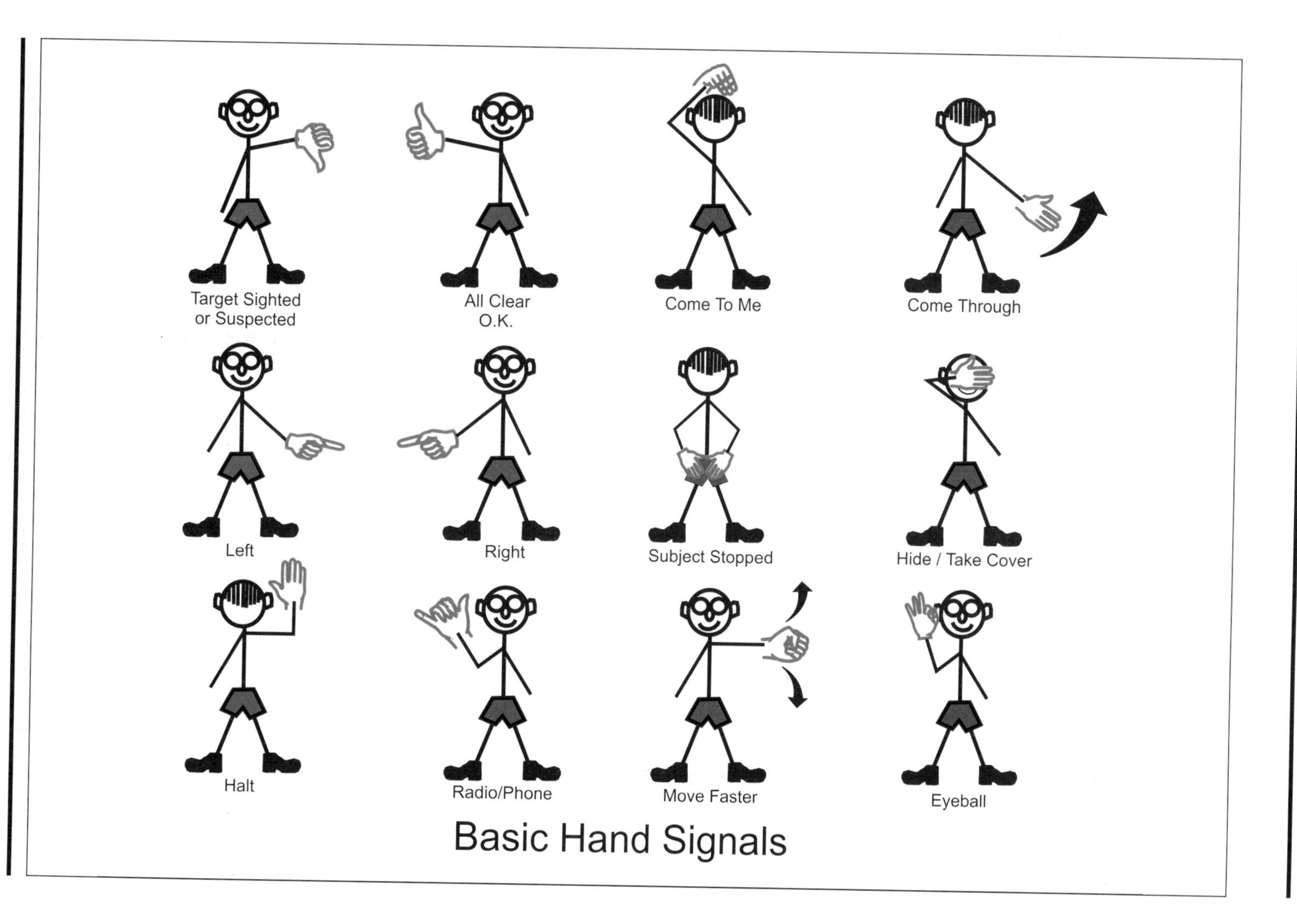
Target Sighted
or Suspected
All Clear
O.K.
Come To Me
Come Through
Left
Right
Subject Stopped
Hide / Take Cover
Halt
Radio/Phone
Move Faster
Eyeball
Basic Hand Signals

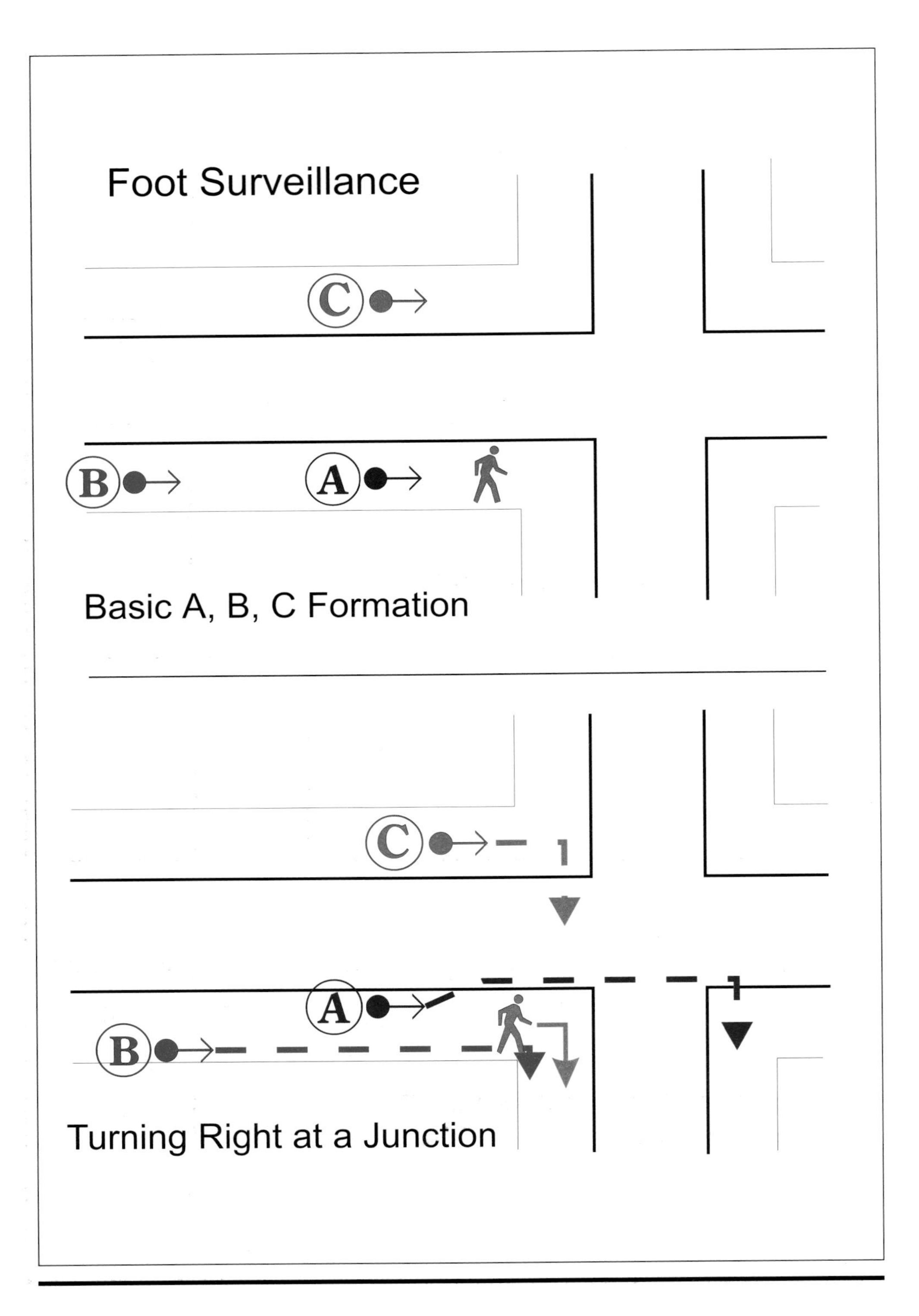
Foot Surveillance
C
B
A
Basic A, B, C Formation
C
1
A
B
1
Turning Right at a Junction

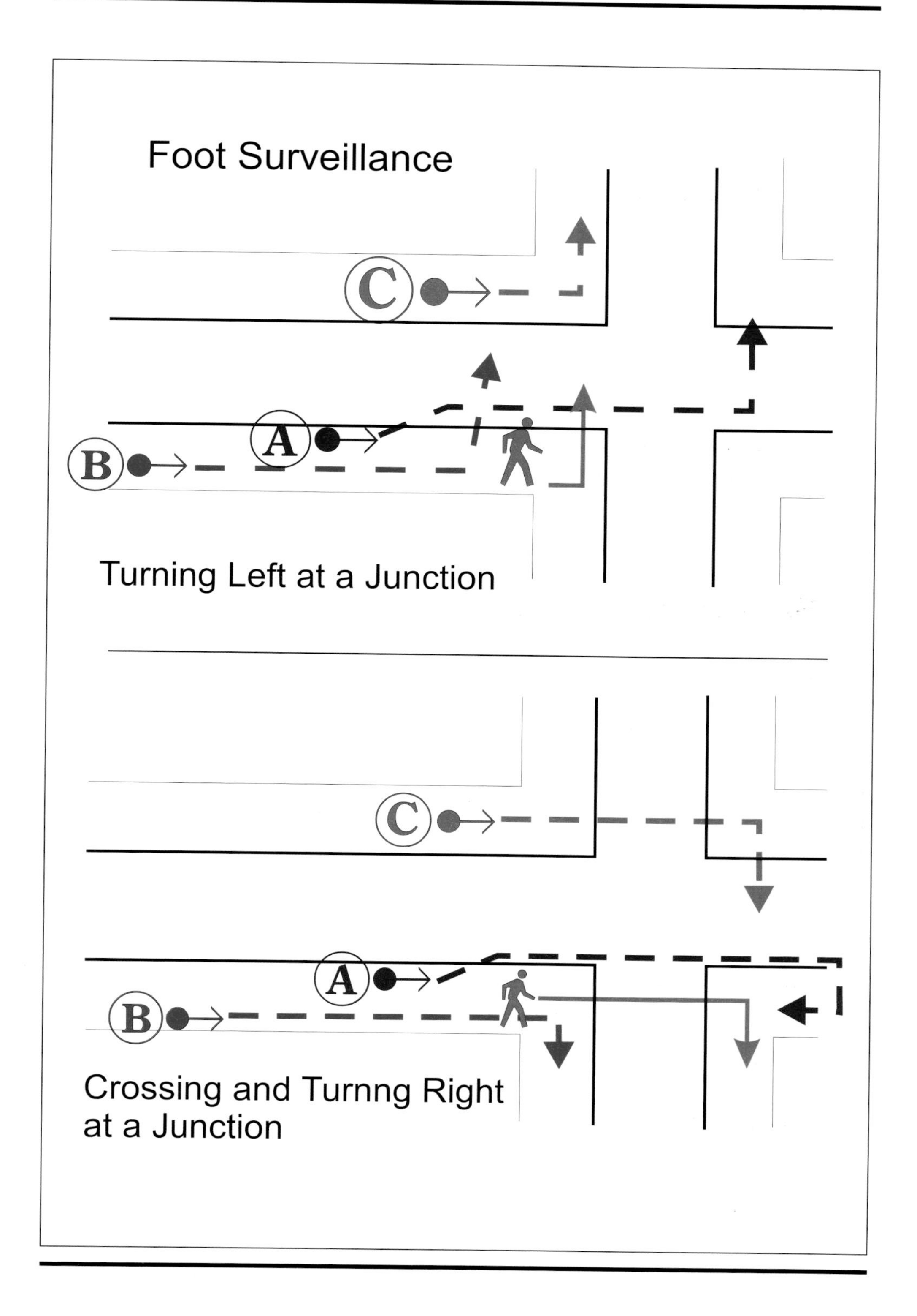
Foot Surveillance
C
A
B
Turning Left at a Junction
C
A
B
Crossing and Turnng Right
at a Junction

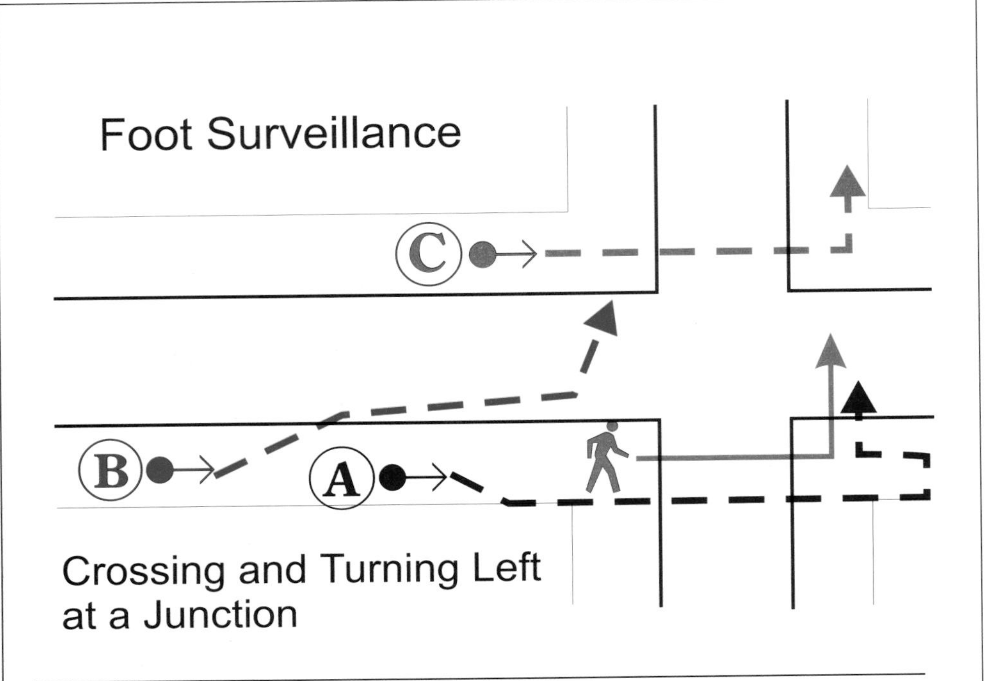

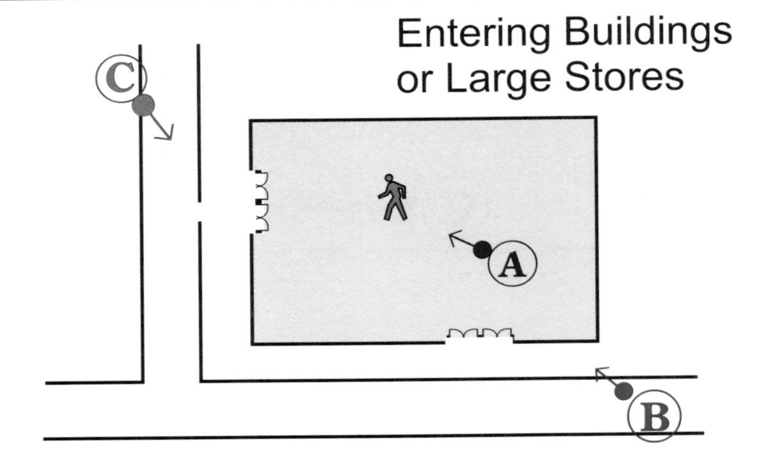

When the subject enters a building or large store, the team must deploy to cover the exits and the subject should be kept under control at all times. Should the Eyeball require a change over, he should ensure that back up has control before he leaves the building.

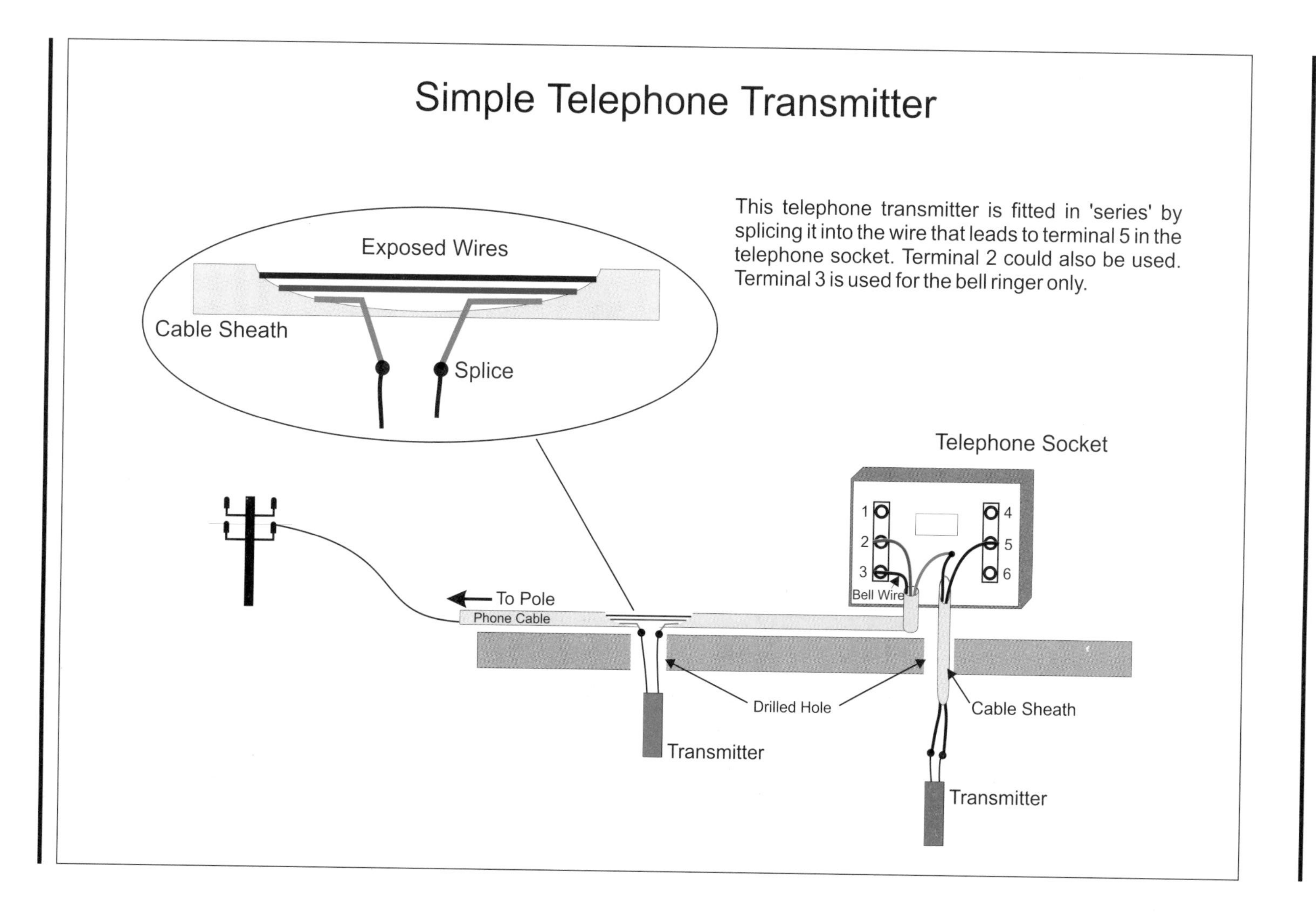
Simple Telephone Transmitter
This telephone transmitter is fitted in 'series' by splicing it into the wire that leads to terminal 5 in the telephone socket. Terminal 2 could also be used. Terminal 3 is used for the bell ringer only.
Exposed Wires
Cable Sheath
Splice
Telephone Socket
1
2
3
4
5
6
Bell Wire
To Pole
Phone Cable
Drilled Hole
Cable Sheath
Transmitter
Transmitter

Domestic Telephone Intercepts

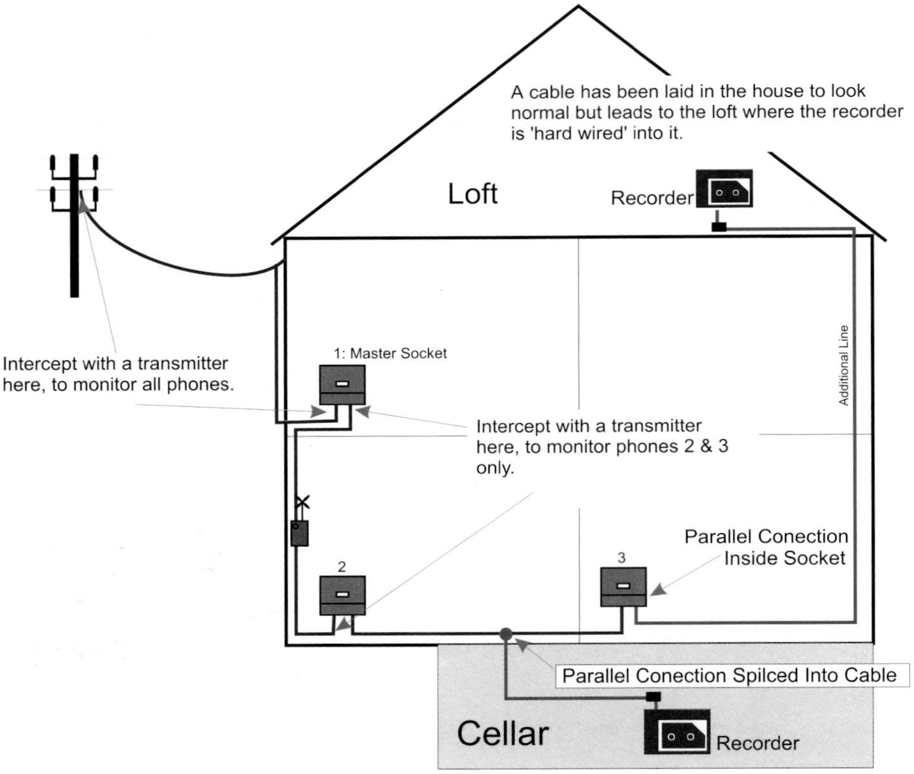

A cable has been laid in the house to look normal but leads to the loft where the recorder is 'hard wired' into it.

Loft

Recorder

Additional Line

1: Master Socket

Intercept with a transmitter here, to monitor all phones.

Intercept with a transmitter here, to monitor phones 2 & 3 only.

2

3

Parallel Conection Inside Socket

Parallel Conection Spilced Into Cable

Cellar

Recorder

A 'hard wired' recorder connected in parallel can be installed anywere along the line to monitor all phones. Additional lines can be laid to ' secure areas' such as a loft, cellar or cupboard where the recorder can be concealed.

Transmitters have to be placed with care if there is more that one telephone on the same circuit. To monitor all telephones the device has to be located between the first socket (Master) and the pole.

Interception of Digital Telephones

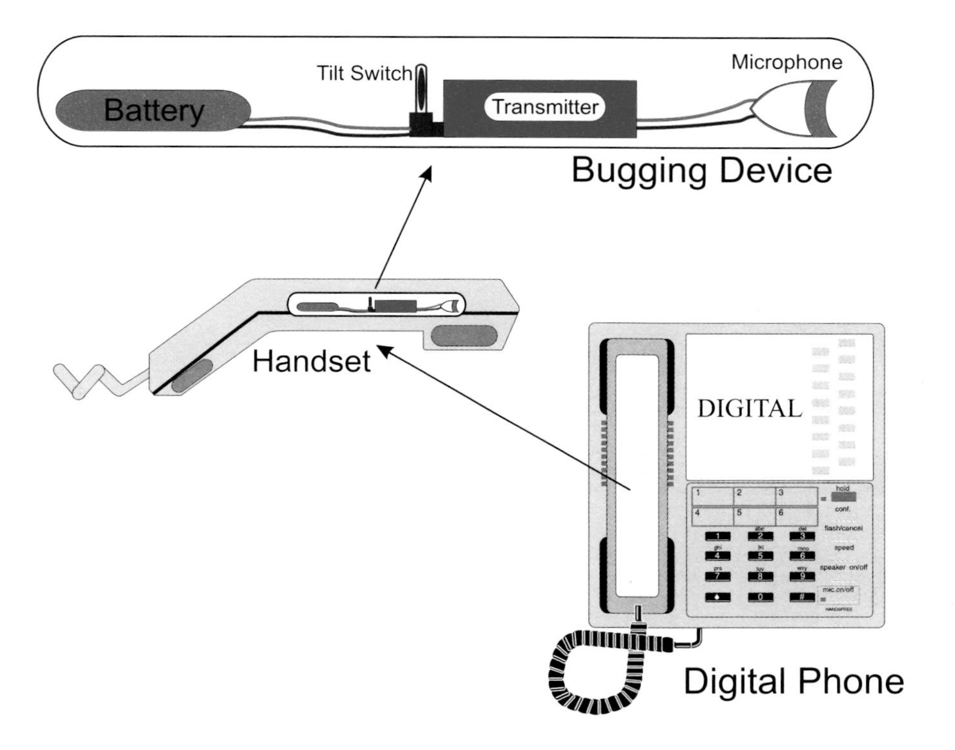

Conventional telephone transmitters cannot be used on digital phones as the conversation signals along the wires are digitised, making them unreadable. Therefore, a conventional minaturised room transmitter is concealed in the handset to transmit both sides of the conversation.

In this simple transmitting unit, the small microphone picks up the voice of the person holding the handset and also the voice of the other person which is heard through the earpiece.

The transmitter is activated by a tilt switch which provides power from the battery when the handset is lifted from its cradle.

Vehicle Tracking Using GPS Satellites

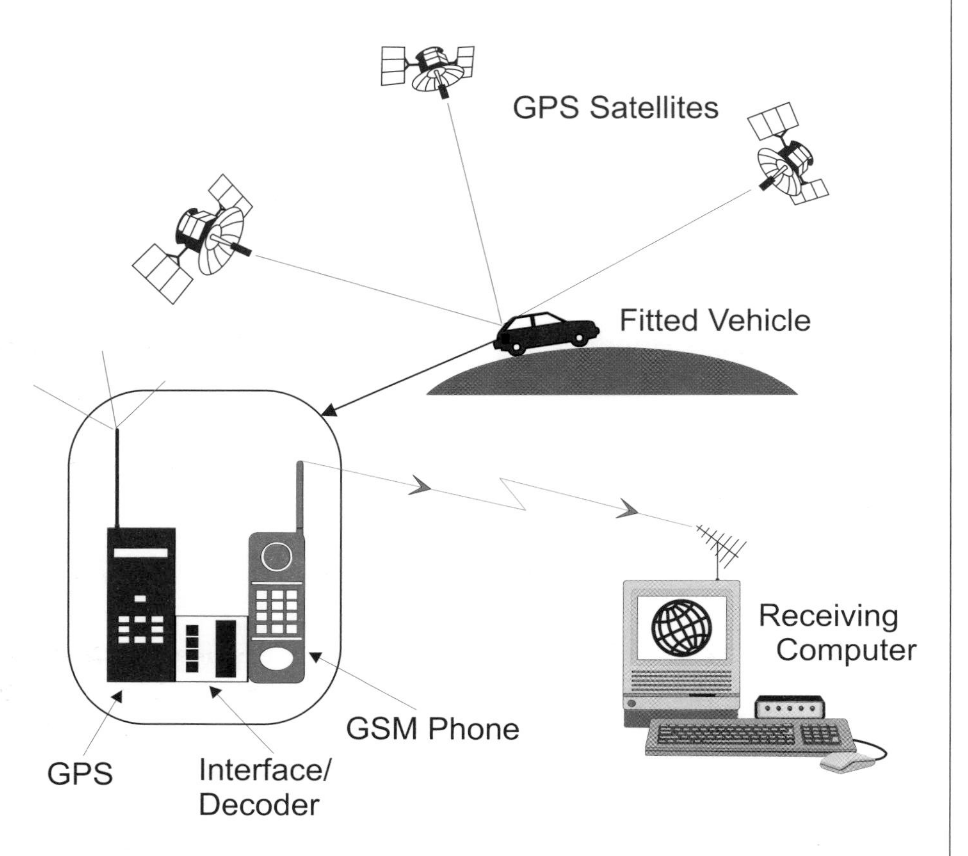

The satellites send signals that are picked up by the GPS receiver to pinpoint its location on the Earths surface to an accuracy of 10 square metres.

The co-ordinates are then converted into signals and are re-broadcast over the GSM mobile phone network or SMS Radio. Theses signals are then received and can be displayed on a computer to provide the vehices location.

The information can be displayed on the computer by digital mapping, accurate Ordnance Survey Grid References or as a Latitude/Lontitude.

Mobile Communications

Identification of Vehicles and Personnel

Many operators and agencies adopt their own style of radio call signs and codes and so there are no hard and fast rules regarding this. Use whatever system you are used to or most happy with.

Tactics

- On the trigger giving a 'STANDBY', all callsigns should acknowledge. No one should be left behind!

- The vehicle nearest the Subject is the 'eyeball' or the vehicle that 'HAS'.

- During the follow, the second (back-up) and third cars will be at the rear, often out of sight.

- The operator in the eyeball vehicle will give radio commentary on the speed and direction of the Subject and of any road hazards.

- Cars will change positions as dictated by the eyeball.

- In rural areas and motorways a greater distance can be allowed between the Subject and eyeball. Cover such as bends, hedges and other vehicles etc can be used. Driver to be alert at all times, looking ahead and reading road conditions and hazards.

- In built up areas and especially busy towns, surveillance vehicles MUST close up and the eyeball should be very close, at times being directly behind the Subject.

- Surveillance car should keep to the nearside of Subject's rear when in close proximity to lessen chance of attracting attention.

- If one has to stop immediately behind the Subject, drive and act naturally. The driver should 'minimise' on the radio and the back-up vehicle should take over the commentary for the time being.

- At night time it is more difficult to tail in country areas without showing out.

- Drive with normal lights, ensure that they all work properly.

If the subject indicates at a junction, do not copy him. If he does indicate, but continues straight, you will be committed to turn.

Mobile Commentary

Whilst carrying out a mobile surveillance the commentary given by the lead car to the other members of the team should be precise, straight to the point and given instantly. Whilst you as 'eyeball' are in front, the remainder of the team may not be able to see the Subject and be some distance behind you.

Certain phrases and descriptions are used to simplify messages and to assist the operators if they do not have any visual contact with the Subject. Although these phrases may appear obvious or unnecessary, they are to assist you and the team to prevent any confusion and subsequent loss of the Subject.

All messages are to be kept short and accurate. A message lasting half a minute could mean that the Subject has travelled half a mile in that time, so do not waffle on. If any operator other than the eyeball wishes to pass a message, he must first seek 'Permission' from the eyeball. Keep your radio microphone held below the level of the dashboard to prevent the Subject from seeing you using it. Should you be directly behind the Subject in traffic, (for example, held up at a set of traffic lights), ask your Back Up to provide the commentary. In a well practised team the Back Up would automatically take the initiative and do this for you.

You should keep the team up to date with an accurate running commentary giving the following details of the Subject's:

- Direction of travel
- Speed
- Intentions to turn (i.e. which indicators used)
- Any deviations made
- Current position in relation to local landmarks (his position not yours)
- Any unusual driving tactics.
- Loss of contact

Direction of Travel

When giving the direction of travel use local landmarks as an aid, street names can lead to confusion if you are not familiar with the area. The direction of travel may be given in the form of;

"He's following the signs marked A629 Halifax..." or
"No deviation, windmill on the nearside..." or
"Continuing straight, no change..."
"He's boxing round to the right..."

Left and Right, Nearside and Offside

When giving any indication to the Subjects movements they should be repeated to make sure that everyone is in the know at once. This eliminates other team members using 'air' time by asking for repeated messages. For instance if the Subject turns Right, he's gone 'Right Right Right'. If he stops he's come to a 'Stop Stop Stop'.

The terms Left or Right should only be used when describing a **turn in direction** and should not be used when pointing out a landmark. For example:

"Subject passing church on the <u>Left</u>"

IS WRONG but should in fact be said as:

"Subject passing church on the <u>Nearside</u>", (or Offside as applicable).

The reason for this is so that any team member, who may be held back in traffic, might possibly be getting out of radio range and can still attempt to catch up with the surveillance by listening to the commentary. Should the radio message be 'broken' and all that is heard are the words 'Church Left' he would presume the Subject has turned Left at the church. Whereas if he only heard the words 'Church Nearside' he would decide to continue straight with no deviation knowing that a landmark (church) had been indicated on the nearside.

Should the Subject use his indicators at any time, inform the team of his intentions, i.e. "Subject's held at a 'T' junction with a nearside indicator". This enables other operatives to prepare for the turn by getting into the correct lane or taking other action. If you are behind the Subject vehicle, which is at a junction or crossroads and indicating to turn, **do not** indicate yourself. Should the Subject decide to drive straight across at the last second, you will be committed to making that turn, which you will have to take in the event that the Subject is observing you and carrying out anti-surveillance.

Advance Warnings of Obstacles

Should there be some form of obstacle to your front such as a set of traffic lights or a roundabout, inform the other team members, i.e. "approaching a roundabout / crossroads / set of lights etc". This will allow them to close up and to prepare to change over as lead driver. Also warn the team of obstructions such as road works, tractors, cyclists and pedestrians etc.

Traffic Lights

On approaching traffic lights, pass all relevant information back to the team regarding their state. The other members may be required to accelerate to catch up so as not be held by the lights. Let the team know the sequence of the lights as they change, and the Subject's position in the queue of traffic. 'Tail End Charlie' should inform you of his position and when he is through the junction.

Speed & Lanes

Relay the speed of the Subject frequently, but more especially when the speed changes. Inform the team in which lane he is travelling, (such as motorway or dual carriageway), or on approach to a junction or roundabout with more than one lane.

Reference Points

As the Subject vehicle passes identifiable landmarks ***(reference points)*** the Eyeball should inform the remainder of the team. For example *"passing church on the nearside"*.

These reference points should be prominent to the operators as they pass them and they will be able to establish how far the Subject is ahead of them. This way they can decide whether to close up or hang back as necessary. **Do not** use moveable objects as reference points (i.e. *"passing Telecom van on Nearside"*), as it will have probably moved by the time the last man gets to it.

Pylons provide a good reference point to indicate the subject's location as they can be seen by the team from a distance.

Roundabout Procedure

When the Subject approaches a roundabout, the team must be given plenty of warning in order for them to close up, especially if the roundabout is busy. The position of the Subject must be given as he approaches the roundabout, when he is on it, when he passes exits and most importantly, when he exits off the roundabout.

In a similar fashion mentioned earlier, when referring to using the terms Left Left as opposed to the Nearside, we adopt a similar procedure to identify which exit the Subject has taken off a roundabout. This procedure avoids confusion especially if a team member is having difficulty receiving the radio commentary.

If we suggest that the Subject vehicle is onto a roundabout (as shown in the colour diagram) and he takes the third exit (Right) the mobile commentary would be as follows:

> ***"He's onto the roundabout, wait"***
> ***"Not One, Not One",*** as he passes the first exit.
> ***"Not Two, Not Two",*** as he passes the second exit.
> ***"Taken Third, Third and Right, A629 Leeds",*** as he takes the third exit.

The team should 'close up' at obstacles such as roundabouts.

You will notice the change of tense between using the terms **One, Two, Three** and **First, Second, Third**. Each exit is numbered in a sequence of One, Two, Three etc. as the Subject passes it, but if he takes a particular exit the tense changes to First, Second, Third etc.

This system was devised in the event of poor communications. If a team member was having difficulty receiving the commentary but heard *"Second, Second"*, he would automatically know that the Subject has taken the Second exit whereas if he heard "Two, Two" he would know that the Subject had passed option two and was continuing round.

The Subject Stops

Whenever the Subject vehicle stops, the eyeball must at ONCE transmit the message "STOP, STOP, STOP on Nearside (Or applicable)". Although the 'Eyeball' vehicle may have to keep moving and pass the Subject, it is important that the other vehicles stop quickly or take appropriate action. If the Eyeball has had to overtake the Subject, the back-up vehicle naturally then becomes 'Eyeball' and the third man as Back-up etc.

The eyeball can give a commentary on the Subject's actions if he gets out of his vehicle and the team leader can decide on what course of action to take, such as put a footman out. Whilst the commentary is being given, the previous lead car should take a position in the event the Subject decides to continue on the original route, back up should take the eyeball and the third man cover the reciprocal route.

Every situation is different but the main aim is for an operator to re-trigger the surveillance and the other team members to cover the possible routes the Subject may take.

The Cul De Sac

The Subject may drive into a cul de sac to either visit an address or to carry out a counter surveillance manoeuvre. Two scenarios can be envisaged - when you know that the road is a cul de sac, or you have been caught unaware and do not realise that it is a dead end until you are into it.

The following actions can be taken when the Subject turns into a cul de sac:-

The cul de sac is recognised as being so

- The Eyeball is to continue straight past the turning and check if there are any routes out at the rear by car or on foot.

- Back-up to carry out a drive past of the turning to identify where the Subject has stopped.

- The third man to enter the cul de sac to positively identify where the Subject has stopped. This can be done either by driving in or by going in on foot. He is also to take up a new trigger position if possible.
- The team reorganise to pick up the Subject when he goes mobile again.

The cul de sac is not recognised until you have turned into it

- Don't panic and act naturally.
- Consider if doing a three point turn and driving out will arouse suspicion. If possible do this out of sight of the Subject.
- Park on the road side and walk away from your vehicle out of sight.
- Drive onto a residents driveway and make a pretext call at the front door. You can then depart, driving out of the cul de sac.

Loss of Contact

Losing contact with the Subject of a surveillance is inevitable from time to time. The type of Subject who is expected to be followed will undoubtedly attempt to lose the tail.

Losses occur for many reasons, e.g. traffic congestion, busy roundabouts, traffic lights and lack of concentration. When this occurs the surveillance team must adopt a search pattern. It assists greatly if the operators draw on knowledge and background of the Subject in an effort to pick him up and continue the surveillance.

The longer the Subject has been 'unsighted', the further your Subject is getting away from you and the more difficult your task becomes in picking him up. As soon as the Subject becomes 'unsighted', even if temporarily, inform the remainder of the team.

When a **"total loss"** is given by the eyeball, the following procedure should then be put into action:- The eyeball will state where the total loss occurred then a search pattern should be adopted as follows with a sense of urgency:-

1. Eyeball to continue in the original direction, looking left and right.
2. Backup vehicle to take first nearside turning after point of loss.
3. Third vehicle to take first offside turning after point of loss.
4. Fourth vehicle to remain at point of loss and check immediate area.

Common sense should prevail as to the time and distance traveled along these routes. If you feel happy that the Subject has not taken your route, you should inform the team leader, return to the point of loss and continue searching in that area or in another that has not yet been checked.

If the Subject is located, the operator should give loudly and clearly 'CONTACT, CONTACT' on the radio followed by the location, speed and his direction of travel.

Keep it in mind that some of the team members during their search may now be out of radio contact and so the location and direction of the Subject should be repeated over the air. Other team members should relay messages if necessary or revert to their mobile telephone.

Never let over-enthusiasm of not wanting to lose the target result in 'showing out' and compromising the surveillance.

Multi-Storey Car Parks

When the Subject drives into a multi-storey car park, the following is a suggested procedure:

1. Eyeball vehicle to follow the Subject vehicle into the car park.

2. Back-up vehicle (if possible), drop off footman to take eyeball on the Subject as he goes on foot (foxtrot).

3. The same vehicle, having relinquished eyeball, will continue to keep observations on the Subject vehicle.

4. Back up, will enter the car park and check for vehicle exits, with a view to plotting up and following on departure. If possible, park near the exit outside the car park.

5. The eyeball footman having made contact with the Subject in the multi-storey will remain with him and follow him into the street where he will be assisted by other footmen who have deployed.

6. The third man remains outside the car park and acts as a shadow vehicle to assist the footmen.

7. Vehicle in the multi-storey is to pick up footmen if the Subject returns to the car park.

8. Remember to examine the Subject's vehicle for the amount of time parked and note anything of interest possibly left on view inside the vehicle.

Motorway Driving

Since the innovation of the motorway, its use has given the criminal a much greater scope of travelling to different parts of the country in a relatively short space of time. It is with that in mind that we have to realise and appreciate the problems that motorways and motorway service areas can present.

Speed

The change from rural and urban driving to motorway driving is obvious and it must be appreciated that we can travel a long distance during a matter of minutes at high speeds. Therefore it is important to be able to correctly assess and judge the speed of the Subject vehicle, in order that the convoy does not become too 'strung out'.

Because motorways stretch for many miles, the eyeball can be retained for longer periods by the same vehicle but only when there is cover of other vehicles and nothing has happened which has caused the eyeball to 'show out'. Each vehicle in the convoy can allow a greater distance between one another and from eyeball to Tail-end Charlie the distance can be as much as a mile or more, so long as radio reception is still good, there are no road hazards imminent and all the vehicles have the power to close up when required.

Speed indication should be given often on the Motorway. Should the Subject increase his speed from 70mph to 90mph, you may find that the rear surveillance vehicle is having to do 100mph in order to close up. This is given as an example only and not intended to entice anyone to speed.

Mirroring

As with urban driving it is important for the eyeball on a motorway surveillance to make sure he does not 'mirror' or copy the actions of the Subject vehicle. Should the Subject pull out and enter another lane, the eyeball should maintain the same speed but remain in his same lane until such times as it appears safe to move out into the same lane as that of the Subject. If you think ahead and decide that the Subject is just overtaking another car and will soon pull back into the nearside lane, then stay where you are for the time being.

Motorway Signs and Marker Boards

Describing terrain and 'reference points' when travelling on a motorway can sometimes be rather sparse. Bridges and National Grid pylons can be used as reference points as they are high up and can be seen from a distance.

As the exits from a motorway appear, we are given warning of these by directional signs which are placed at one mile and half mile intervals (in some cases 2/3 and 1/3 mile) prior to the exits. Each of the exit warning signs detail the distance, junction number and road classification number coming up.

You must bear in mind that vehicles on motorways can only go ONE way until such times as they get to exits. If the Eyeball on the motorway becomes too close (as often happens with slow moving heavy Subjects) they should overtake the Subject and position themselves at the next exit in order to get behind him as he passes. At this junction the operator must also prepare for the Subject leaving the Motorway here also.

Never simulate a breakdown on the hard shoulder in order for the Subject to overtake you, (for you to get back behind him), you will be noticed.

- **Approaching Junctions**

At motorway exits, the Subject's position in the road in relation to the countdown markers and his speed, must be given quickly and often.

On approach to a junction, the Eyeball should always give prior warning and the team should close up. On passing the countdown markers the Eyeball should be giving a fast commentary as he approaches each, stating the lane that the Subject is in and his speed.

For example:

"1 mile marker board, junction 36, centre lane, speed seven zero (70)"

"1/2 mile marker board, junction 36, Leeds A622, nearside lane, speed seven zero (70)

"Countdown markers, three hundred nearside lane, two hundred, nearside indicator, one hundred, gone left, left, left at Junction 36"

Or

"Countdown markers, three hundred centre lane, two hundred centre lane, one hundred still centre lane. Committed, Committed, continuing straight". *If the Subject does not deviate and continues on the motorway.*

Motorway Service Areas

These areas usually have a large cafeteria and service areas, and give access for members of the public to park their cars and seek refreshment before continuing their journey. Because of the proximity of the parking areas to the motorway and the possibility that a Subject can change the direction he is travelling by using the service roads, we have to cover the options which are open to him by deploying the various operators in the following positions.

Motorway service stations are a popular R.V. for those under surveillance and the team should be deployed to maximum effect.

Upon entering a motorway service area:

1. Eyeball should take the Subject onto the service area and keep watch on him, commentating on his activities to the rest of the team.

2. Back up vehicle should go onto the service area and park on the same car park as the Subject. He should then go out on foot to assist and take the eyeball.

3. The vehicle in position three should come onto the service area and take up a position to cover the Subject moving off in his original direction (back onto the motorway), normally in the area of the fuel station.

4. The first vehicle can then remain in the service area and locate the service road which may take vehicles onto the other side of the carriageway. Service roads sometimes have barriers across them and are used for maintenance vehicles, Police and hotel users.

5. The original eyeball vehicle will be responsible for picking any footmen.

6. The motor cyclist or any other surveillance vehicles can be used at the team leaders discretion, to cover any other deviations from the service area. He may require the motorcyclist to take up position on the other side of the carriageway in the event the Subject takes a foot bridge across and meets with others on the other side.

Driving At Night

When driving at night, it is very difficult for the subject to identify the vehicle or occupants in the car behind. As the following cars headlamps are so bright, we tend to be blind to anything but the lights themselves and so in busy times such as 'rush hour' we can afford to get closer to the Subject's vehicle.

Conversely, in rural areas any surveillance car will soon be spotted at night and it may not be practical to 'hang back'. Ensure that the change over of surveillance vehicles is carried out frequently and always in the mirror of the Subject. Vehicles turning off may satisfy the Subject's curiosity.

Make sure that your side lights and head lights are all working properly. A faulty light will soon be noticed.

On long, open roads, you can afford to give the Subject some distance.

Log Writing

Obviously a record of events should be made during a mobile surveillance as they would if you were on a 'static'. Use of a dictaphone is ideal as you can give a running commentary, making note of times and events taking place whilst on the move. It is not wise to write up your log sheet whilst in the middle of a surveillance at a temporary stop, in the event that you may miss seeing something. Save the writing up of logs and reports back at your base.

When back at your base, plot the Subject's route on a map. This will reveal any patterns or unusual routes that the Subject has taken.

CHAPTER EIGHT

Foot Surveillance

Get to your business - Spy!

Rudyard Kipling
from the 'Spies March'.

A good standard of foot surveillance by an operator or team can only be acquired by constant practice and experience.

Difficulties will most certainly occur when carrying out a foot surveillance if there is a lack of communication between the team. Without radios, confusion arises and the likelihood of a loss of contact or actually 'showing out' is very high.

Covert radio equipment is essential and communication with each other is paramount.

The Surveillance Operator

As previously mentioned, the ideal operator could be described as being the **'Grey Man'** or

Mr. 'Nobody' but a Mr. 'Everybody' who looks like Mr. 'Average'.

A good dress sense is required and should be governed by the fashion in the area that you are working in. No flashy clothes, identifying ties, badges, or extravagant jewellery etc.

Never wear bright clothing but always carry a change of clothing with you, i.e. jacket, hat, bags, etc. A plastic carrier bag in your pocket can be used to put your jacket in, thus changing your overall appearance. Do not walk in an upright, purposeful posture but be relaxed and casual.

If possible, use a vehicle to 'back' the footmen.

The use of disguises are NOT recommended. An alert Subject may notice a characteristic of an operator and any change of appearance would only help to confirm any suspicions.

A change of outline is recommended, i.e. removal of hat or scarf, the putting on or off of a jacket, plain glass spectacles, or putting your hands in pockets, etc. Do not wear sunglasses unless everyone else about you is also wearing them.

Always carry an amount of change and money with you. If the Subject gets onto public transport or takes a taxi he will have to be followed. If he enters a pub or cafe you may also have to go in with him.

Surveillance Team Formation

When the Subject departs on foot or leaves his vehicle, the surveillance team has to act with urgency in order not to lose contact with him at this critical stage. Prior to the surveillance commencing, the team leader should have planned and briefed his team what to do, in the event that the Subject goes on foot.

If the team is involved in a three car follow and the Subject parks up, then walks into a town centre, a foot operator should deploy straight away to take control of the

Subject. The remainder of the team can then position their cars for the departure and then join to 'back' the Eyeball on foot.

At times the footman will have to 'dump' his car and risk parking fines or wheel clamping. If at all practical, another operator can move the footman's car to a safer location for him.

Deploying on Foot

When deploying on foot remember:

- Think before you deploy. Ask yourself, 'Is it necessary, do I have to get out?'
- Never screech to a halt. Act naturally and never run or appear to rush.
- Always reverse park your vehicle to enable you to manoeuvre away quickly.
- Cover up any equipment, paperwork or maps.
- Inform the Team Leader of your intention to go on foot.
- Switch your main radio off and your covert set on.
- Don't forget your mobile phone, you may end up on a train!
- Ensure your car is locked, have some money with you.
- Carry out a radio check with your covert radio set.

'Reverse Parking' enables you to depart quickly, without having to manoeuvre first.

Back Up

Once the team is deployed on foot and has control of the Subject, one of the operators should remain with his vehicle in order to act as Back Up for the team.

Not only can he pick up and re-deploy any footmen but if the Subject gets into a vehicle or onto public transport you still have a mobile option.

The Follow

Three Man Team (A, B, C Method)

A foot surveillance team requires the mobility and the frequent changing of its operators. The basic formation of a foot team can be two or ideally three operators, who for diagrammatic reasons we refer to as **A, B** and **C.** and is therefore known as the **A,B,C Method.** The formations and method are shown in the colour diagrams.

In diagrammatic form, the formations appear regimented and give the impression that the positions have to be strictly adhered to. This is not so, as once on the ground, the experienced operator will take up his position without thinking. The use of three men in a team permits greater variation in the position of operators and also allows for a member who may be getting 'warm'. He can then be replaced by another operator from the team. It reduces the risk of losing the Subject and affords greater security against showing out.

Foot surveillance is about team work and communication. If you lose sight of the Subject, another team member should automatically take control. There will also be pedestrians in the area to provide you with cover. On the ground you have to make constant appraisals as to the Subjects intentions and always think to yourself, **What If..**

What if he crosses the road...

What if he enters a building...

What if he turns and walks the other way...

The A,B,C system is easily controlled and practical in a location such as this.

The A, B, C Method under normal conditions is as follows and is represented in the colour diagrams:

(A) The **'A'** or lead position is behind the Subject with a reasonable distance between them depending on cover, crowds and the area.

(B) The '**B'** operator is on the same side of the road and is following the operator in '**A'** position and concentrates on keeping '**C**' in view. There is no need for '**B'** operator to have the Subject in view.

(C) The **'C'** operator is positioned on the opposite side of the street from the Subject and is slightly behind the Subject.

The combination of operators and their respective positions will alter according to the geography of the area and will alter many times during the course of a follow.

The A, B, C Method in very crowded streets is difficult to adhere to and at times it is advisable for all three operators to be on the same side of the street. The leading operator should follow very close to the Subject to observe his every movement.

The A, B, C Method on a street with little or no traffic provides greater difficulties and it is necesary for only one operator to be on the same side of the street as the suspect and the other two operators on the opposite side. If a vehicle is used as back up, a footman can be picked up and re-deployed ahead of the Subject if need be.

Use of Cover

It cannot be stressed enough that when following a Subject on foot, the surveillance team should use every available cover afforded in the street at all times. Cover can be a parked vehicle, a bus stop, a lamp post, park bench, tree, pedestrian, in fact anything which momentarily can completely or partially hide the operator should the Subject turn around. Do not duck and dive into doorways or behind lamp posts but act naturally at all times.

Never follow a person whilst looking at the back of their head. Should they suddenly turn around you will make eye contact. Always look at the feet or waist.

During surveillance training courses, we have found that one of the hardest things for the students to do was to stand still. If the Subject had entered a store, one of the team has gone in with him, leaving the other two outside to cover the exits. The two acting as back up find it hard to keep still without feeling obvious. If there is a shop doorway, stand to one side of it as if you are waiting for someone and stay there rather than keep shifting about. If there is a seating area or bench then sit on it, they are natural places for you to remain static. In addition, if there is an empty phone box near by then get into it.

Team Replacements

It must be realised that the closer the operator is to the Subject, the more likely he is to be seen and recognised, therefore, he must be changed often. The larger the team, the more changes can be made, but do not make changes for changes sake. It is the operator in the lead position who will decide when to change.

Communications

Communications can literally make or break a foot surveillance. A foot team should normally carry covert radio sets. In addition they should know and be familiar with basic hand signals.

During surveillance training courses we carry out a foot exercise and allow the students to use covert radio sets. They appear to do reasonably well, except for dropping their heads onto their chests in order to speak into the concealed microphone. This is not necessary as you can talk quite openly whilst acting normally.

After about an hour, we relieve them of their radios and watch their foot surveillance turn into chaos as the students struggle to communicate. They find it difficult to act naturally as they did before, as they are having to concentrate and think much harder .

When you are close to the Subject, such as in the same room or in a lift, remember to remove your covert earpiece as sound can sometimes be heard by third parties. When speech is not practicable, for instance you may be sat beside the Subject in a cafe or you may be sat on a bus when it is difficult to use the radio, a procedure known as the **'Click System'** may be adopted.

This system enables you to communicate by pressing the covert microphone (PTT) switch a given number of times, in answer to direct questions received. The receiving radio receives and hears these presses as 'clicks'.

The system is as follows:

1 click on PTT = No	**2 clicks on PTT = Yes**
In excess of 3 clicks = All standby	

The amount of clicks may differ from organisation to organisation: some adopting two clicks for NO and three clicks for YES. Use whatever you find easiest but ensure that the whole team is aware of the system that you are using. **Remember, you can only ask direct questions which require a Yes or No answer.**

The Team have to take tight control of the Subject in a large car park. A footman should be deployed ASAP or the Subject will be lost.

Tactics in Foot Surveillance

A surveillance operator is a member of a team and he must at all times be in communication with the others. In the event of radio failure, use simple hand signals that are unobtrusive and discreet and which have been pre-arranged with the other members of the team.

The use of these signals and tactics must be automatic and apply to every team member.

When on the ground consider the following:

- Avoid eye to eye contact with the Subject. If approached, never act surprised.
- Always remember that you may be seen but not necessarily noticed, therefore act naturally at all times.
- Should you be approached, think to yourself, what is my cover story?
- Always ask yourself, am I in the right position? If not, get into it.
- Do not dodge behind corners or into shop doorways if the Subject turns round, this only attracts attention. Use shop doorways, etc. as cover when you cannot be seen by the Subject. Do not forget that shop windows can reflect the activity of persons on the opposite side of the street. They can be of use to you but they can also be of use to the Subject.
- Always act naturally if the Subject turns round and retraces his steps, walk on and avoid eye contact. Remember, another team member should automatically take control.
- When in a confined area always endeavour to be doing 'something' but act naturally.
- In crowded areas, walk on the outside of the pavement. This gives better vision and less obstruction. The nearside of the pavement is good cover when the streets are less crowded.
- Do not take unnecessary risks.

Cafes & Public Houses

If the Subject goes into a cafe you must decide whether to follow him in or not, remember, he could be meeting someone. If you decide to go in, it is suggested that two people go in (preferably a man and woman) to make your presence appear more natural.

Attempt to get close as possible to the Subject, (if necessary), without being obvious and sit opposite your partner. You can then talk on a radio giving the appearance that you are in conversation.

- Do not feel awkward in public places, you have a right to be there, you are a member of the public.
- Always have cold drinks. If the Subject suddenly leaves, it may appear odd for you to leave a hot drink or meal on the table and walk out.
- Sit close if a meeting is in place, you do not necessarily have to face the Subject.
- Go in with a female partner.
- Use the crossword page of a newspaper to write on and make notes if necessary.

Department Stores and Supermarkets

Should the Subject enter a department store be aware of both uniformed security guards and store detectives. They are trained to recognise anything out of the ordinary or suspicious and they will soon notice you if you do not act naturally. Many store detectives make use of covert radios and you will soon become the Subject under surveillance, in addition it is likely that you will be tracked by closed circuit TV.

Be extremely careful if you enter a store with a bag containing a covert camera such as a sports bag. Store detectives will naturally 'lock' onto anyone entering a shop carrying a bag, for obvious reasons.

When the Subject enters a building or a large department store, the team must deploy to cover all the exits out. The Subject should still be kept under control visually until all the exits are covered. Should the 'eyeball' require a change over, he should direct his back-up to the Subject by radio before he leaves the building.

Telephone Kiosks

Telephone Kiosks can be used at any time by the Subject or yourself for various reasons:

BY THE SUBJECT

- The obvious - to make a phone call.
- To perform anti-surveillance
- To get out of the weather, i.e. rain & wind whilst waiting for someone.
- To receive a phone call from an associate.

The eyeball must always be wary of any stop at a telephone kiosk. The Subject, even if making a call, has a clear view to three sides and it is a natural tendency for him/her to look around outside whilst talking on the phone.

Always check the box when vacated. He may have left a scrap of paper with a number on or the message received.

BY YOURSELF

- Use the box as natural cover from where to observe.
- Act naturally and pretend to speak.
- If there are two boxes adjoining, can you get into the second box and listen into the Subject's conversation? If you do, place your back towards him, don't let him see your face.

If your subject does not drive, or does not even own a car, prepare to deploy an operator on a bus.

Buses

Should your Subject get onto a bus, attempt to sit behind him so that he does not have you in his view. If he goes upstairs, remain downstairs at the rear (unless there is a strong possibility that he may meet someone on the bus).

If you have your back-up following you in a car you will need to communicate with him. If the bus is crowded you may not be able to communicate with your covert radio and so you will have to resort to the 'Click System'. Your back up will only be able to ask you one way 'Yes' or 'No' questions, as you will have to answer with the correct clicks as previously mentioned.

For example:

"Is the Subject sitting upstairs?"	**'Click, Click'**	(Yes)
"Are you upstairs?"	**'Click'**	(No)
"Can you trigger him off the bus?"	**'Click, Click'**	(Yes)

Trains

Should your Subject arrive at a train station, the team leader will decide whether to put an operator (or two) on the train with him. The size of the surveillance team will obviously dictate on what course of action to take. If it is envisaged that the Subject is likely to use a train, or that it is part of his routine is to do so, you can be better prepared and deploy a larger surveillance team.

If the Subject alights a train, the difficult part is when he arrives at his destination, he could get into a taxi, walk, get a bus, or be picked up.

On entering the station and ticket office, the following should be adopted:

- The Eyeball gets right behind the Subject at the ticket counter (if the destination is unknown). He is to establish the Subject's destination by overhearing the Subject or by 'blagging' it out of the counter assistant.
- The 'eyeball' purchases a return ticket to the Subject's destination and informs the team of the details by radio.
- The ticket is passed to a second operator who gets on the platform/train with the Subject and takes the eyeball. He keeps the Subject in sight at all times.
- The team leader should decide whether to put a second operator on the train. Remember the Subject may get picked up at his destination or jump into a waiting taxi.

- The mobile units deploy, one unit heading for the trains destination (if practical), and the others make their way to the major stops along the route. (The Subject may get off the train en-route, especially if he is surveillance conscious).

Following a Subject on a train is fairly simple as he has no where else to go. The difficult part of the surveillance is when he arrives at his destination as so many options are open to him. He could continue on foot, get into a taxi, jump on a bus, or be met and be driven away etc.

Lifts & Elevators

Should the Subject go into a lift, a foot man could possibly follow him in, but keep in mind the following:

- Is it necessary? The operator will have to pull off the surveillance afterwards as he has been too close.
- Is it safe or wise to enter with him?
- Remove your covert earpiece.
- Avoid eye contact at all times.
- Take control of the button panel. If you do, you can ask the Subject which floor he wants, (as any person would do), you then get off at the same floor or the one above or below.

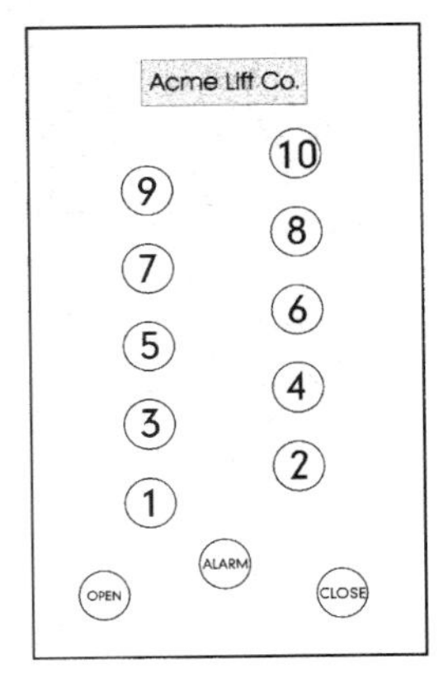

- Be prepared for casual conversation with others or the Subject himself.
- Relay the floor to other team members as soon as possible.

If the Subjects intended floor is unknown (as he has taken control of the button panel) your best option is to take the second to top floor if he is going up. This way you will be able to identify which floor he gets off at. Should he not have got off by the time you reach your floor, his only options are to get off at the same floor as you, or the only one remaining which is the top floor.

Note Taking

During a foot surveillance it is difficult to make written notes of the Subject's movements, locations and contacts etc. Therefore either carry a dictaphone or relay all events to your Back-up in order for him to log them.

Foot surveillance is similar to mobile surveillance but can be even more difficult if there is a lack of communication and the Subject can easily be lost. The team should rotate positions as circumstances dictate and take advantage of structural and geographical cover in the area. If the Subject turns on you, react spontaneously but more importantly, **act naturally**.

If you are carrying out 'Personal Injury' type surveillance, and the Subject enters a supermarket, you have to go in 'fast and close', with your covert video to obtain valuable evidence.

CHAPTER NINE

Observation Posts

> *These are the names of the men which Moses sent to spy out the land. And Moses sent them to spy out the land of Canaan, and said unto them, 'Get up this way southward and go up into the mountain'.*
>
> *'And see the land, what it is; and the people that dwelleth therein, whether they be strong or weak, few or many'.*
>
> ***Book of Numbers, Chapter 13***

Much surveillance work involves a static surveillance in order to carry out a continuous watch on an individual, a premises or objects. The static Observation Post (O.P) could be tasked to observe a warehouse to note all deliveries made, or to watch a private house to photograph the occupants when they leave. The reasons for carrying out a static surveillance are many and the methods used to carry out such a surveillance are described in this chapter.

In addition, the static O.P. may purely be used to provide a trigger as previously discussed. The surveillance van, (if used as an O.P.), can follow on behind a mobile surveillance (or even take part in it, if used carefully), and move into a new static position when the subject arrives at his destination.

What is an O.P.?

- A static position from where you can observe, report and photograph activity.
- It can be Covert or Overt
- Long or Short Term.
- Urban or Rural.
- Located in buildings, vehicles or rural 'hides'.

An 'urban room' O.P. in a dis-used office.

Individual O.P. Tasks

The principal tasks of an operator in an O.P. are to:

- **Observe** - to observe and watch events.
- **Record & Photograph** - to compile logs and photograph/video activity.
- **Operate Radio** - to relay incidents to the mobile teams or team leader.
- **Sentry** - to warn of unwanted visitors to the O.P..

An experienced and well trained operator will be able to do all of these tasks to enable a minimum of two men to run the O.P..

Manning Levels

The O.P. should be manned by a minimum of two operators. Manning levels should depend on:

- Time spent in the O.P.. (hours, days, etc.)
- The aim of the O.P..
- The size of the area to be kept under observation and the amount of activity to be recorded. One may watch and photograph whilst the other records and reports by radio.
- The size of the O.P. site. Is there enough room for a team?

Why Do O.P.'s Become Compromised?

On occasions, rural and urban O.P.'s will become compromised by either the Subject or unconnected Third Parties. The reasons for compromise are many, but we can minimise the risk of compromise if we look at the reasons why the O.P. is brought to another persons attention.

Operators Own Fault

- Movement - the biggest giveaway.
- Noise.
- Smells.
- Smoke.
- Torch Light.
- Lack of Camouflage.
- Tracks To and From the O.P.
- Seen During the Insertion, Extraction or Re-supply.

Others Fault

- Accidental finding by Third Parties
- Purpose finding by suspicious/curious Third Parties
- Children Playing
- Dogs and other animals

What to do in the event of a compromise

- Be absolutely certain that you have been compromised.
- Wake those who are sleeping.
- Inform your Back Up. They may need to extract you, cause a diversion or intercept those who have spotted you.
- Pack items of equipment - quickly.
- Move out (decide if it should be covert or overt), i.e. silently or at the 'crash'.
- Move to the Emergency R.V. for pick up.

URBAN OBSERVATION POSTS

When we speak of urban surveillance we mean any situation where a surveillance has to be carried out that does not involve the techniques described below in the section on **Rural Surveillance.**

An urban surveillance can take place in a village, town, city, industrial estate or housing estate, in fact any where that is built up. Obviously rural techniques can be deployed in an urban situation but the type of O.P.'s used in an urban situation are different.

The urban static O.P. can take the form of many guises, the main two being the **Surveillance Van** and the **Room O.P**. Other types of O.P. can also be used and are discussed later in the chapter.

INDOOR STATIC O.P.'s

The indoor or 'room' O.P. can be any form of building or structure from where you can carry out your observations such as:

- Hotel room.
- Disused office.
- Portacabin.
- House.
- Factory/mill/warehouse.
- Shop.
- Boat.
- Garden shed.
- Loft space.

In fact anywhere where you are not in a vehicle or hedgerow/undergrowth.

In the past we had to establish an O.P. to observe an inshore oil tanker ,which would moor up along a river quayside. There was no where to carry out observations from apart from an old schoolhouse, (used for storage) , located on a neighbouring companies premises.

Our client was granted permission for us to use the old school house. Once inside, it was found that there was no upper flooring in the building and so we hired a scaffolding tower from a builders merchants in order to provide us with a viewing platform. The tower was approximately 40 feet high and we were able to view out of a 'crucifix' window and through holes made by removing roof tiles.

From the top of the platform we were able to covertly observe, photograph and video record the events that took place below us.

This disused chapel was used as an O.P. site.

Operators were able to observe from the crucifix window down onto the subject premises.

Inside the O.P.

The interior brickwork had to be chiseled away to provide a wider viewing area, without altering the exterior appearance of the crucifix.

A scaffolding tower was hired and erected inside the chapel to provide a solid viewing platform.

Observations were maintained by 2 operators, for up to 6 hours, in total darkness.

SELECTION OF A Room O.P.

• Ensure that your routes in and out of the O.P. are protected from view. Insertion and extraction are the most vulnerable times when you are likely to be seen. Have your Back-Up positioned nearby, it may be necessary for them to cause a diversion during this time.

• Make sure you can see the subject and the Subject's approaches. Many room O.P.'s are situated on upper floors and over look the subject.

• Ensure that you will not be seen whilst observing. People in adjacent buildings, especially if they are higher up will overlook you. Site your observation position as far back from the window or viewing aperture as possible.

• Do not silhouette yourself by having a light background behind you or a window behind you. If the room is darkened wear dark clothing, and make a dark background by hanging a length of dark material behind you.

• If possible, fix net curtains over the windows, if not, a cloth screen hung between you and the window (a few feet back and not covering the window itself) will provide you with cover and slits can be cut, for observation. House plants on a window sill do not look out of place, which will also provide you with 'natural' cover.

• Have an escape route planned in the event you need to leave the O.P. quickly.

• Check if there is a power supply to recharge batteries, toilet facilities and water.

VEHICLE O.P.'S - SURVEILLANCE VANS

As described in the chapter on Surveillance Equipment, a fully equipped surveillance van is worth its weight in gold to the surveillance team. Having the ability to move your O.P.. into a position, observe and photograph the Subject's and then depart without arousing any suspicion from the subject or locals, is paramount to a covert investigation.

It is difficult to sit in the front of your car on a housing or industrial estate and carry out observations. It is extremely difficult to last for any length of time before you are reported to the Police or arouse third party suspicions. With an increase in crime rates, the general public are normally on their guard to anything suspicious.

Occasions do arise when it is necessary to observe for long periods from a car and the operator can feel exposed and uncomfortable when doing so. If you have to, try and sit as far from the subject as possible, preferably having to look obliquely at the Subject rather than straight at it. Use any cover that may shield part of the car such as walls, hedgerows and trees. If you are sat in the passenger seat this will give the appearance that you are waiting for the driver to return. If sat in the rear, use a jacket on a hangar to provide you with some cover. Many motor accessory shops sell small roller blinds that attach to car windows to act as sunshields. These are effective for providing temporary cover, especially when attached to the rear windows of the car.

What if I am challenged?

Should you be challenged by a member of the public, have a good cover story prepared and make it sound convincing. This could be anything from carrying out a traffic survey to actually telling them that you are an investigator. Obviously you would not do this if you have the trigger but if you are acting as back-up and away from the subject area you may need to do so, especially if you will be operating in the area for a number of days. On occasions, it may be worth telling the curious person that you are waiting to 'serve' divorce papers on a person and you are waiting for them to return home etc.

VEHICLE O.P.'s (The Van)

You do not always have to be close to the subject's address in order to provide the 'trigger'.

During your pre-surveillance, you decide that the only way to observe the subject premises is by use of a surveillance van. The vans position is important and you must decide whether to observe though the rear window or through the front and sides.

When positioning the van, consider:

- Your O.P. position in relation to the subject, can you see the subject clearly, are there likely to be any obstructions. Can you identify who leaves the property and in which vehicle.

- Is your position obvious.

- If the subject goes 'mobile' are you able to give directions of travel to the remainder of the team.

- Do you intend to join the team and follow the subject when he leaves? If so, does the van need to be facing in the intended direction.

- Are you in a cul-de-sac with only one escape route. If so, park facing outward in the event you have to extract quickly.

- Is it feasible to self extract or is it too risky and so you have to be driven out?

The Insertion

If possible park the vehicle where there is some cover from the view of others, especially in residential areas. If you have to park outside a house (e.g. a semi-detached or terraced) then park between the two properties. One neighbour will think that the van is connected with next door or vice-versa and so possibly limit suspicion about the van.

If it is difficult obtaining a parking position, it may be necessary to park the van or another vehicle the day before the surveillance to 'reserve' a space. If a car is used it can be driven away to make a space for the van the following morning. If it is not possible, you may have to wait for residents to depart for work and then jump into their parking space.

Before moving into position carry out a recce by driving past in another operators car rather than using the van. Carry out a foot recce if required, find the most suitable spot to position the van so that you get the best possible view. Note anything about the subject premises; are they occupied, what vehicles may be parked out of view, is there milk on the doorstep, are any windows or curtains open etc.

Moving into position can be done in one of two ways. You can either have a partner drive you into position and then lock the door and walk away from the vehicle, or you can drive yourself in and then hop into the rear of the van. Obviously the first choice is recommended and much safer. Should you be seen to crawl into the rear of the van, the surveillance would be compromised before it has even begun.

Always leave the ignition key in a place under the dashboard or in the glove compartment where you can easily reach it if you have to depart from an area quickly. A team member should also carry a spare set that he uses during the insertion and extraction.

The Van O.P.

When the surveillance is being carried out in what would be termed as a 'risky or hard' area, back up and radio contact between operators is essential. At any sign of compromise or trouble then it would be wise to terminate the surveillance and leave the area.

In the past, the following encounters and problems have occurred when using surveillance vans:

- Neighbours stood beside the vehicle discussing its presence.
- Arrival of Police after being called by suspicious neighbours.
- Curious people attempting to look into the one way glass.
- Children playing and shaking the vehicle in an attempt to set off the car alarm.
- Tyres being deflated by playing children.

- The vehicle being accidentally being blocked in.
- Attempted break-in of the van.
- Many parking tickets issued whilst an operator is in the rear.
- A ladder on the roof rack, (placed as part of the cover), being stolen.

You may be working on an investigation where you will only get one chance to watch for the information that you need, and so remaining in position is vital. However, the safety of the operator should be paramount and the surveillance terminated should any problems occur.

Once in position you can set up your O.P. for your requirements. Start the surveillance log detailing as much information about the Subject area as possible. Set up the video camera on its tripod, set camera for correct exposure and focus, adjust any other special equipment that you may need and have it organised so that you know where it is when you need it. Inform the team leader when you are established and report anything of interest.

If there is no activity, report a 'No Change' to the team leader every 20 minutes or so.

AMOUNT OF TIME SPENT IN THE O.P

Once set up in your observation van you can be totally self contained and remain there for as long as you wish. It is not uncommon to find observations being carried out for periods of twelve hours or more and takes a committed operator who can cope with the demands of the task whilst being in a confined space with long periods of boredom.

Should the O.P.. be in for long periods, you can either change the operator and his vehicle or just change the operator and use the same vehicle. When a change of operator is made it is better done by driving out of the position, making the change and then returning. Whilst the change is being made, a third operator should move into the same spot to take a temporary trigger and to reserve the parking space if need be.

Should there be some local information to pass onto the 'fresh' operator, you can brief him during the time away from the Subject area.

On one surveillance task in the past, a van was used for a period of three weeks to observe the comings and goings from a house in Lancashire. The residents of the street appeared to not notice the van but the Subject gave it more than the occasional glance a few times. One morning, when it was known that one of the Subjects would leave the house, the rear doors of the van were left open with a number of cardboard boxes in the back for him to see.

The Subject had seen us moving the boxes about and this hopefully satisfied his curiosity. After he had departed the cardboard boxes were flattened and the observations of the house continued from the rear of the van.

A view from inside the surveillance van.

VEHICLE DISGUISES

For most purposes a plain unmarked van is sufficient to carry out observations from. Should you feel the need, then it can be disguised in a manner of ways:

Magnetic signs advertising a fictitious company, (e.g. Joe Bloggs Plumbers, etc), are useful and can be attached and removed within seconds. It would not be wise to have a fictitious address on the sign in the event a suspicious person decides to check it. A mobile telephone number would not seem out of place and could be included on the sign. Should anyone be suspicious of the vans presence, they may telephone the number written on the side of it. If they do, an excuse can be given as to why it is in the area and you will also know that certain residents are aware of it being there.

Fitting the van with a roof rack holding a ladder or copper pipes, gives the van an appearance of having a purpose and so people would not think twice about its presence. If you do this, make sure they are secure and are not prone to being stolen!

USE OF VAN IN MOBILE SURVEILLANCE

Should the van be used as a static O.P. or trigger and thereafter be used as a mobile unit, caution should be taken not to 'show out' and the vehicle should be used as little as possible.

Should the van be required to act as a trigger or move into a position to obtain evidence later on in the surveillance, it should remain at the rear of the 'convoy' until required.

> *On an investigation involving personal injury fraud, we had to establish that the Subject was physically able to drive a car. (She had suffered a broken wrist and had a neck injury due to a road traffic accident).*
>
> *Using the surveillance van with an operator in the back, the van was driven in front of the Subject and she was 'followed' from the front. Video film was obtained of her being able to drive competently. She was shown to be able to steer, change gear and indicate during busy town centre traffic thus disproving her claim of a neck and wrist injury and being unable to drive.*

THE ROOM O.P

The indoor room O.P.. is used less often than the surveillance van as it is not always possible to obtain a position from where the Subject can be observed. However, when carrying out your pre-surveillance, always consider the static O.P.

RURAL SURVEILLANCE

On occasions, a surveillance operation may be required in a rural setting such as having to watch a farm, or a premises located in the countryside. If the use of an observation vehicle is not practical then the task still has to be continued. To establish a watch on the subject it may be required for the operator to be totally camouflaged and concealed in his local surroundings for sometime to achieve his aim. You do not necessarily have to be in the countryside to mount a rural O.P.. The techniques and methods described below are equally useful in cities or towns when the only position to carry out observations from may be a hedgerow, undergrowth or a small wood.

In the recent past we have carried out many surveillance tasks, which required complete camouflage, three of them were in urban areas such as Salford, Bradford and Chester. It may appear that it is verging on the extreme to be adopting these methods, but at the end of the day it is a means to an end. If you can achieve a result by photographing a subject and the only way of doing so is by lying on your stomach in a hedgerow, then that is what is to be done.

Personal Qualities

For obvious reasons, this type of task is suited to someone with experience and more likely to be someone with a military background or who has had the relevant experience.

Personal camouflage is essential to the surveillance operator, as much as it is to the professional soldier.

Some of the information in this chapter is taught to infantrymen during their basic military training where it is essential that these methods are adopted, to ensure their own personal survival. For the investigator, (who is possibly less experienced) they are paramount to ensure his remaining undetected.

CAMOUFLAGE AND CONCEALMENT

Camouflage and concealment is probably the most important factor in this type of covert role. You may be positioned within 10 metres or less of your subject and be required to take photographs.

Your subject should not have any indication of your presence, and this should be done by blending in with your surroundings. Camouflage and concealment is an art which requires much practise and experience

If we look at the reasons why we see things and what brings them to our attention, hopefully, we will be able to counter them, and thus make ourselves become less visible.

- **SHAPE**

  Your body shape or outline is distinct and has to be 'broken down' to look more like a blob than that of human form. The head, neck and shoulders being the most important. This can be done using some form of camouflage netting attached to a camouflaged bush hat which hangs and drapes over the shoulders to break up the outline.

  Should you be using camouflage netting to make a hide, the outline should also be broken down with natural foliage. Attempt to break down any straight lines that occur.

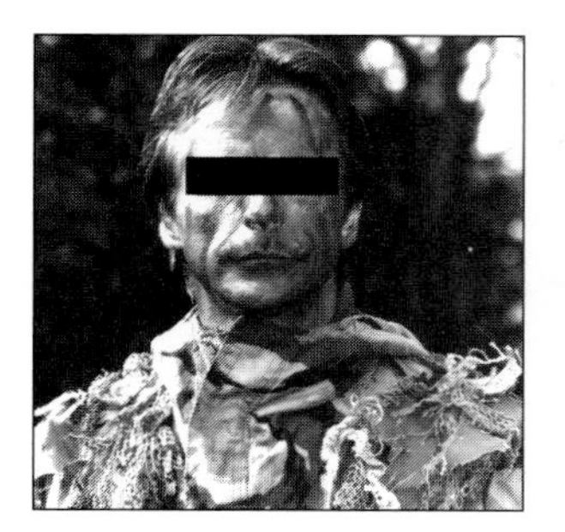

Various stages of personal camouflage

Concealment: Blending in with your surroundings

• SURFACE

Many objects have a smooth surface but bushes and grass are irregular, therefore a camouflage jacket on its own may not be enough cover in order for you to blend in. By attaching irregular pieces of camouflage material to it you can give its surface an uneven texture. Local foliage attached to your person also assists in the breakdown of the surface and helps blend in with the surroundings.

Smooth surfaces are often reflective which means they shine. Obviously anything which shines will be instantly seen. Shiny objects to be aware of are; camera lenses, binoculars, watches and jewellry. The forehead, face and hands also shine so make use of camouflage cream/paint (cam-cream).

Camera lenses and optics should be fitted with lens hoods or attach a fine cloth mesh over the lens to reduce reflections.

• SILHOUETTE

When moving to and from the O.P. position and when in the position itself attempt to keep below the horizon to avoid being silhouetted. When moving, make use of cover such as hedgerows and ditches, or crawl if necessary. When using cover to observe, attempt to look through the cover or around it rather than over the top. Make use of cover behind you to prevent you from being silhouetted.

This Arctic patrol stands out, as the men do not blend in with their background and they are too evenly spaced.

• SHADOW

Make use of shadow for cover whenever possible. It is difficult for an observer to see into shaded areas. Make sure that your shadow does not betray you.

• SPACING

Avoid any areas that provide isolated cover. A single bush in a field may seem an appropriate spot to observe from but it will stick out like a sore thumb becoming obvious. Areas such as this are more difficult to move in and out of and occupy. If there are a number of you having to move across country, vary the distance between you so that the line appears irregular, try not to 'bunch up'.

• MOVEMENT

Movement is one of the most important give-aways to your presence. You may be totally camouflaged in your surroundings and made to be invisible, but a slight movement from the hand or a turn of the head will catch someone's eye and you will be compromised. If you have to move, move slowly, deliberately and with stealth.

CAMOUFLAGE PAINT & FACE CREAMS

In order to camouflage the face and hands 'cam cream' will have to be applied. Cover the whole face, forehead, neck, ears, hands and wrists with a thin base layer of brown cream so not to reveal any patches. Then sparingly apply more cream in dark patches at random to break up the shape of the face and possibly add a touch of dark green coloured paint. Remember to do the 'V' of your neck and the back of your wrists, otherwise clothing will ride up and expose skin.

Put on personal camouflage after the 'drop-off' and before inserting the O.P. Do not forget to apply 'camouflage cream' to all exposed parts!

People with black or dark skin should also apply cam-cream as the skin reflects light and becomes shiny, cam cream should be non-reflective.

COMMUNICATIONS & HAND SIGNALS

When working in an O.P. during daylight, silence is essential and so communication may be achieved by using hand signals. Hand signals may be used when communicating over a distance and an explanation of each is illustrated in the colour diagrams.

When using radios, it is essential that you have communications with your back up. At times you will be lying very low on the ground or in ditches below ground level, therefore radio signals will be reduced. A 'mag mount' antenna attached to a hand set should be used to maximise communications and should be elevated if possible by putting it up a tree or attaching it to a fence post etc.

THE RURAL OBSERVATION POST (O.P.)

When conducting a pre-surveillance, you may decide that the only way to conduct static observations would be from a rural point of view, i.e. carry out observations from a hedgerow running alongside a perimeter fence or from a small wood adjacent to the subject.

Remember, that these types of O.P. require much personal discipline. The operator has to work for long periods, often lying down, motionless, in poor weather and in uncomfortable conditions. Your personal camouflage and the concealment of the hide has to remain paramount to avoid detection. You may not always have the advantage of having natural cover immediately available and may have to create your own in the form of a hide.

You have to pick your point of observation carefully, taking the following into consideration:

1. From the O.P. do you have a good view of the subject area? There is no point in having an excellent O.P. position if you cannot see your Subject.

2. Do you have a good view of the Subject's approaches? This is important if the subject goes mobile and gives you those extra seconds you may need to have your camera up and running or to radio your team.

3. Is the position obvious or are you overlooked? Do not choose a position where you stick out like a sore thumb, always be aware of being overlooked by buildings or from hillsides. In addition you should have a clear view of the approach to the O.P. in the event passers by become too close.

4. Is your route in and out covered from view? This avoids casual observers wondering where you are going to and from. Choose your route tactically, keep to hedgerows, banks, ditches and railway tracks and avoid crossing open spaces.

5. Where can you R.V. in case of compromise and where can your back-up be positioned? Should the O.P. be discovered and the O.P. party have to split up, then you need an emergency rendezvous where you can meet up again or be picked up.
Your back-up needs to be positioned where he can get to you quickly, with his position also being safe from suspicion.

6. Is there provision for a rest area in the location? If you are in a two man O.P., it may be practical to have a rest area to the rear where one man can sleep and eat whilst the other is observing etc..

7. Allow for any special equipment that may be required, (i.e. enough video batteries or night vision aids). You may find yourself in a confined space, so take only the equipment that is necessary for the task.

8. How long will it take to move into position and to establish the O.P.? Consider if you are moving at night, add plenty of time to move in and establish the O.P. before your task should begin.

9. Note any particular hazards. The possibility of dog walkers or farmers in the vicinity, also wildlife and farm animals - cows are very curious and will crowd you, whilst sheep will scatter! Familiarise yourself with landmarks and features on the route in to aid navigation at night.

10. Carry out a radio check to your back-up location, you must have communications.

The Recce

Carry out a day and night time recce if necessary. If you have to walk about during the daytime in unusual surroundings then adopt an identity to suit. Walking dogs is ideal cover or wear running clothes as if you are orienteering/jogging. Wear a fluorescent jacket as if carrying out a road survey etc. All circumstances differ so use your imagination.

Avoid wildlife and farm animals - cows are curious and sheep scatter.

The Insertion

Allow plenty of time to move into your O.P. position. If establishing the O.P. at night let your eyes get accustomed to the dark before setting off. If you have to be in position before first light allow enough time to set up and establish the O.P. and check its concealment.

Move in with caution, at all times you must:

1. Remain alert, stop frequently to look and listen. Do not cross open spaces but keep to hedgerows and wood perimeters to give cover. Move slowly, thus creating less noise. Should you have no option but to cross a field, move singly, keeping your body as low as possible and crawl if necessary. Remember, your silhouette will betray you.

2. Maintain your sense of direction, use landmarks to navigate by, such as hills, pylons, urban lights etc. Alternatively, use a compass.

3. Make use of surrounding noise (such as cars passing), which will give you cover and distraction when moving. Be extra cautious when crossing obstacles such as roads, bridges, gates or fences.

4. Avoid farm animals and wildlife.

5. Do not take risks, have a plan ready if compromised, keep your back-up informed of your progress. Take note of where you can take cover and hide if necessary along your route.

6. Enter the O.P. from behind keeping the position between you and the subject. Be aware of creating tracks that lead to the O.P..

Establishing the O.P.

Move into the position keeping low to the ground. Once in position remain silent and motionless for a 5-10 minute period. Listen and observe in case you have been seen or followed into the O.P. and get accustomed to the local noises and the area.

Attempt to hollow out the foliage by pushing back brambles etc. If necessary use secateurs to snip at the foliage to make a comfortable observation position. A viewing position may have to be constructed using 'chicken wire' and then suitably camouflaged. If necessary add extra foliage to the outside of your cover. Remember if you intend using the same position over a period of time, you will have to replace the foliage as it dies off.

If you are able, crawl forward of your position and look back to identify any gaps in your camouflage. If you are unable to do this, radio your back-up and ask him to make a pass and check it for you. Establish radio communications with your back up as soon as possible.

The Hide

As mentioned, the O.P. can be in a variety of places, a hedgerow on an industrial estate, a railway embankment, a ditch at the side of the road or in the edge of a wood. The best position to use will be determined by yourself and the circumstances.

The O.P. may be a short or long term position. In most instances it is possible to construct a simple O.P. using camouflage netting and then covering this with natural foliage as camouflage. If you are in a hedgerow you will have to 'hollow' out a space using secateurs to form your hide.

The 'rural O.P.' Note the camouflage on the camera.

In long term O.P.'s or when there is no cover, a 'hide' may have to be constructed. This type of hide is only mentioned briefly in this book as it requires skill and experience to build one. Very briefly explained, an area of turf is removed from the O.P. site, the ground is dug out to form a hollow and the soil removed from the area, a low roof is then built over the top. The turf and camouflage are replaced on top of the roof and a small entrance is made. The operators can then live in the 'hide' for a number of days without replenishment.

A hide of this sort requires practice and experience to build. Plenty of back-up in the surrounding area will be needed to protect the O.P. team during construction, which is normally done at night.

These type of O.P.'s in the security industry are rare but come into their own when used in bare rural areas to counter the activities of poachers etc.

The Extraction

At the end of the period of surveillance, you will need to prepare to leave the O.P. which we call the **extraction** phase.

You will be required to :

- Pack away all equipment that will not be needed.
- Inform your back-up when you intend to leave, he can then assist by picking you up or by observing the area to give you warnings of third parties.
- Dismantle all camouflage and bring natural foliage inside the O.P. to die. Leave the position as you found it, taking with you all refuse, including all human waste.
- Move out one at a time and never in haste, be as cautious during the Extraction as you would during the Insertion.
- Inform your back up of your progress along the way out.
- If necessary remove cam cream and camouflage clothing. This may be done just prior to the Pick Up.

Care of Equipment

In your O.P., your equipment will be exposed to the elements and dirt. Cameras and radios are particularly vulnerable, so make provision for them to be kept dry and free from dirt. On completion of a task, give all equipment a thorough clean. If it has been damp, air the equipment to dry out, then test it to make sure that it still works. Replace batteries or recharge them if necessary.

Suggested O.P Equipment

Green Waterproof Sheet, Cameras, Radios, Trowel, Small Saw, Chicken Wire, Mag Mount Antenna, Insect Repellent, Camouflage Netting, Secateurs, Green String, Food and Water, Sleeping Bag (one between two), Spare Batteries, Refuse Bags.

Camouflage Equipment

Any piece of equipment, especially binoculars, scopes or cameras, will require some form of camouflage as they will be forefront in the O.P.

Lenses should be covered with some form of fine netting. A green 'cam scarf' obtained from ex-army stores is ideal. Cut a piece to size and retain over the front lens with an elastic band. Also use this material to wrap around equipment or drape over a tripod etc. A piece of black stocking stretched over the lens reduces lens flare and reflections when shooting into the sun, without any considerable loss of light.

Vehicle camouflage nets cut down to small sizes, (6' square), are ideal for quick camouflage when covered with some natural foliage. Items to assist putting up camouflage nets are cord and string, clothes pegs, elastic bungees and extendible fishing rod rests to act as supports.

Logistics

The length of stay in your O.P. will decide on what comforts or necessities to take with you.

Considerations are:

- Food and water - you will need enough for the duration and do you eat hot or cold? Is it tactically safe to use a camping stove, or use special self heating foods such as 'Hotcan'? Take enough to drink and a flask is essential.

- Toilet paper and something to defecate into should be considered. Ziplock type polythene bags are ideal. If the O.P. position is to be used over a period of time, it is unwise to relieve yourself in the position. Take all waste with you when you leave.

- Should you be in the O.P. for a considerable amount of time, you may require a re-supply of food and batteries etc. In addition, you may have to pass on surveillance logs and films to be processed. A system should be planned for re-supply, whereby you may have to leave the O.P. to collect/leave equipment from a pre-arranged location.

- Take enough batteries to supply radios and cameras etc. When used in the cold they have a shorter lifespan.

- Use a sleeping bag - one between two.

An O.P. was once mounted in a freight/storage container such as this one.

THE CLOSE TARGET RECCE (CTR)

The Close Target Recce is a close inspection of a place where the operator has to search and obtain detailed evidence. The operators may have to enter a yard, farm, business premises, garden or whatever to conduct their search and so stealth and slow movement is vital.

A daylight recce of the area should always be carried out to establish your routes in and out, and establish the layout of the subject area to identify any difficulties.

The CTR team should always cover each others movements by moving one at a time and using as much cover as possible. You should always have a back-up ready to cause a diversion or have them extract you should you become compromised.

Make the most of covert equipment such as Night Vision Devices. If you have to obtain photographs, use infra-red film and flash, or use 'Zero Light' video cameras. The CTR is considered a more advanced method of gathering information and is therefore only briefly mentioned.

CHAPTER TEN

Surveillance Photography

This chapter deals with the aspects of still and video photography in relation to surveillance. It is not intended for the reader to become a professional photographer but deals with the various aspects which will enable you to produce a quality photograph which has been taken whilst being in not so ideal conditions, poor light and with telephoto lenses.

If you are watching an individual or premises for a long period of time to obtain photographic evidence, it is imperative that you know your photographic equipment, its abilities and limitations. It can be disheartening and even embarrassing having to report back to a client after twenty hours of observations with a photograph which is either blurred, out of focus or under-exposed.

After you have read this chapter, it would be wise to go out and experiment on a roll of film some of the techniques that have been described. Use your camera's manual to assist you or obtain a photographic book from the local library which will provide you with more detail. It is said that "practice makes perfect" and during a surveillance the situation changes constantly so familiarise yourself with your equipment.

In todays world of investigation the video camera is being used more and more rather than the 'still' camera. Although a still camera will produce excellent results, it requires practise and experience to use it, whereas a video camera can be used by anyone after only a few minutes of handling and practise.

Often you will have to 'brass neck it' - get your camera up and running, or you may miss that vital piece of evidence.

There are many cameras available and choosing one can be difficult. At the end of the chapter you will find a short check list of features to help you decide. Principally a 35mm SLR, (single lens reflex), camera is ideal. Ultimately the quality of your photographs will be a combination of factors; your ability to use the camera correctly, the quality of the equipment, your personal judgement, the quality and type of film and lens that you use.

SLR CAMERAS - MANUAL OR AUTOFOCUS

The majority of cameras now being produced are auto focus, which offers speed and accuracy when focusing on your Subject. It is personal preference which type of camera to use - if you are happy with a manual focus camera then why change?

If you are new to SLR photography this concept could be for you. Having used both systems, the auto focus camera is used for the majority of my surveillance work. Manual cameras are more robust and durable whilst the auto focus cameras are more fragile but offer additional features such as built-in auto-winders, more accurate metering and more compact telephoto lenses.

Not only can they focus more quickly than a manual camera but they can also adjust to keep a moving Subject in constant focus. Having said that, I probably use my auto focus camera on manual focus mode for the majority of the time.

HOW A CAMERA WORKS

A camera is a light proof box with a piece of film at one end and a lens at the other which focuses the light on to the film. The light forms an image which is captured on film.

The amount of light that enters the camera and reaches the film is controlled by two things:

1. **The size of the hole *(aperture)***
2. **The length of time the aperture is held open *(shutter speed).***

Different combinations of these two factors give different effects on film which are very important and are described below.

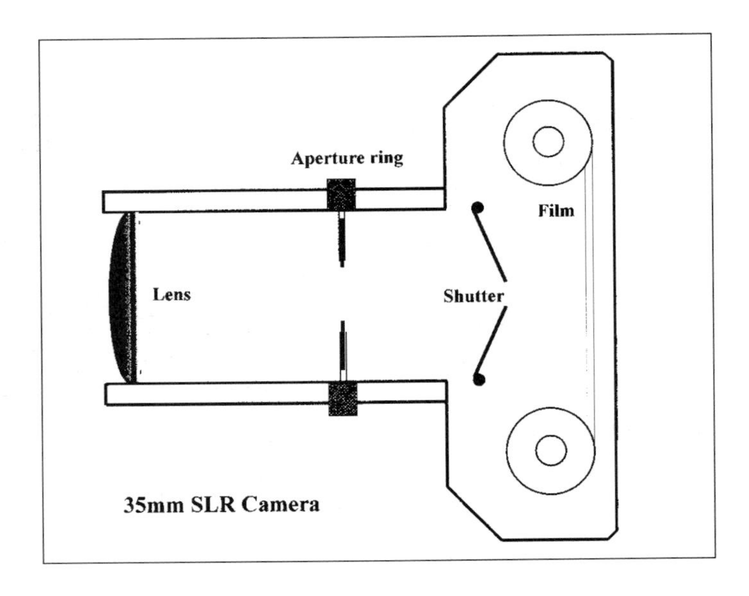

Correct Exposure* is a combination of *aperture setting* and *shutter speed

APERTURE

As stated, the aperture is the size of the hole that allows light to reach the film. The size of the aperture can be altered and is given a value which represents the size of the hole. These values are called **'f'** numbers or **'f'** stop' and follow in sequence:

f 2 2.8 4 5.6 8 11 16 22

f2 being the widest and **f22** the smallest.

The series as a whole is arranged so that each **f** number lets in twice as much light as the previous number. The numbers are always given in the above numerical sequence.

The relationship is shown in the table:

F no.	**22**	**16**	**11**	**8**	**5.6**	**4**	**2.8**	**2**	**1.4**
Units of light	**.5**	**1**	**2**	**4**	**8**	**11**	**32**	**64**	**128**

So why is aperture so important to the surveillance photographer?

A wide aperture such as **f 2.8** will allow in plenty of light and this is what is required in a low light situation, which is common in surveillance photography.

It would not be viable to set the cameras aperture to **f11** on a dull day as you will require the maximum amount of light possible to give you the correct exposure.

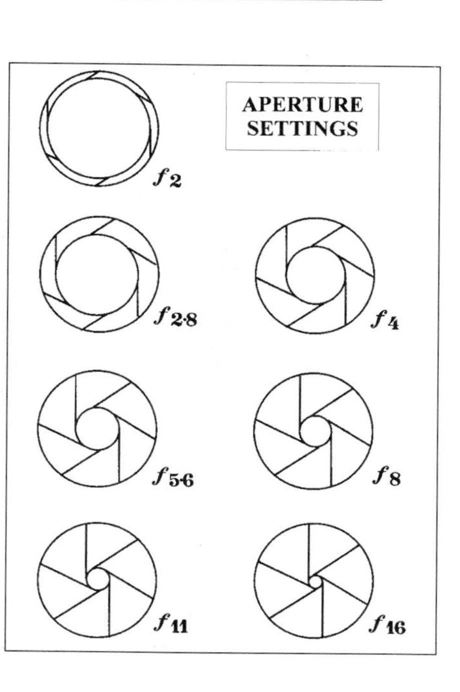

SHUTTER SPEED

Shutter speed is the amount of time the shutter is held open to allow sufficient light to fall on the film.

Shutter speed is calibrated and measured in fractions of a second i.e.

1/15 1/30 1/60 1/125 1/250 1/500 1/1000 1/2000

They are similar to the aperture **f numbers** in that each speed either doubles or halves the one next to it.

As we said at the start of this chapter, a correct exposure is a combination of **aperture setting** and **shutter speed.** On average a setting of **125/250th** is the norm.

EXPOSURE MODES

Many cameras have different exposure modes and your cameras' manual should explain what modes are capable of. A number of the following modes should be available to most cameras.

- **Automatic Exposure (also called Program).**
- **Aperture Priority.**
- **Shutter Priority.**
- **Manual.**

AUTOMATIC EXPOSURE (PROGRAM MODE)

Most SLR cameras have an Automatic or Program mode as it is often called. When in this mode, all that is required is for you to point the camera, which takes its own meter reading. The camera calculates the amount of available light and automatically sets the cameras aperture setting and shutter speed to obtain a correct exposure. This is not always ideal in surveillance photography where more control over the camera is required in different situations, therefore shutter priority and aperture priority are discussed at some length.

Let us imagine that you have just taken a meter reading and your camera suggests an exposure of **1/125** sec at **f8.**

To achieve the same exposure you could use any of the following aperture and shutter speed combinations:

2.8	**4**	**5.6**	**8**	**11**	**16**
1/1000	**1/500**	**1/250**	**1/125**	**1/30**	**1/15**

The combination you choose depends on the Subject being photographed, as all the settings are relative to each other, however, the resulting picture can appear different.

APERTURE PRIORITY MODE

When in this mode, the camera takes a meter reading and then adjusts the shutter speed according to which **f** number it is set at.

i.e. If aperture **f16** is manually selected, the camera may automatically choose **1/15** sec.

If the aperture is set manually to **f2.8** the camera then chooses **1/1000** sec to obtain the correct exposure.

In surveillance photography, this mode should rarely be used except when **Depth of Field** is important, such as taking pictures of:

- Landscapes - large areas.
- Shooting through fences or dense foliage.
- Buildings - pre- surveillance.
- Aerial photography.
- When you need to place Subject in its surroundings.

Depth of field is explained later in the chapter, but we tend to use this aperture priority mode in poor light so that the widest aperture can be set on the camera, this in turn will automatically set the fastest shutter speed possible.

SHUTTER PRIORITY MODE

In this mode, a desired shutter speed is manually selected and set on the camera, i.e. **1/250** sec. The camera meter then automatically sets a suitable aperture.

Your choice of shutter speeds affects how moving Subjects will appear in the picture. Slow shutter speeds such as 1/30 or 1/15 of a second, will blur moving Subjects. Fast shutter speeds such as 1/250, 1/500 or 1/1000 of a second, can be used to freeze the action of a moving Subject. **Fast shutter speeds are required when using telephoto lenses to prevent camera shake.**

MANUAL MODE

This mode is used when you require full control over exposure. Photography in this mode would only be recommended in surveillance circumstances to the experienced photographer.

DEPTH OF FIELD

Depth of field describes the extent of the picture that will be in focus at a given **f** number.

In theory, only the Subject on which you focus is completely sharp and 'in focus', but an area of acceptable sharpness also lies in front of and behind the Subject. This area is called the 'Depth Of Field'.

As the size of the aperture decreases, the depth of field lengthens, bringing more of the picture in front and behind the Subject into focus.

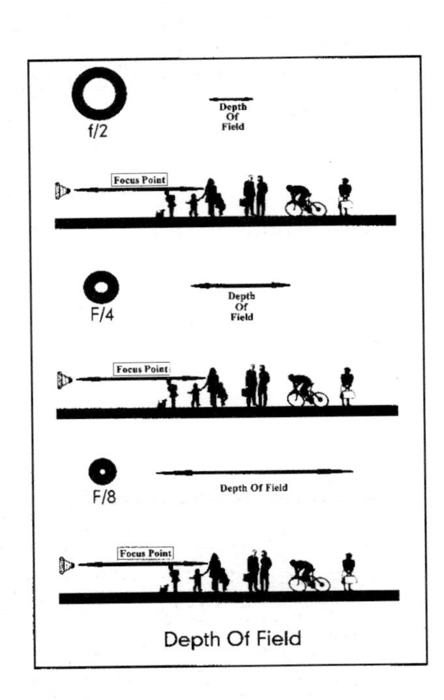

Depth Of Field

The size of this depth of field area varies and depends upon three factors.

- **The focal length of the lens.**
- **The aperture the lens is set to.**
- **The camera-to-subject distance.**

Depth of field can be used when you need, to photograph a person where the background is important and is also required to be in focus.

Using Depth of Field

By using the camera's aperture correctly, you can make the wire fence (left) become 'invisible' (below).

Conversely, if you require a photograph of a person but need to keep the background/foreground out of focus, such as taking a picture of a figure through a wire fence, you do not want the fence appearing in the photo and obscuring the Subject. Therefore use a large aperture, which will limit the depth of field making the fence invisible in the picture.

SHUTTER SPEED AND TELEPHOTO LENSES

When using telephoto lenses, fast shutter speeds should be used to prevent image blur caused by camera shake. Camera shake is much more apparent with long lenses - in addition to the picture being magnified so camera shake is exaggerated. Whenever using telephoto lenses try to use a support or tripod. If the camera has to be hand held, use the following table as a guide to which minimum shutter speed to select, to prevent image blur.

For every **mm** of focal length lens used, use a like shutter speed.

Lens	Minimum shutter speed
35mm	1/30 sec
50mm	1/60 sec
100mm	1/125 sec
210mm	1/250 sec
300mm	1/250 sec or faster
500mm	1/500 sec or faster

In poor lighting conditions you will not always be able to obtain an ideal shutter speed, i.e. if the weather is very dull, you have a 300mm lens fitted to the camera, the camera's exposure meter may tell you that a speed of 1/125 sec is required. If this is so, either use a support or try to hold the camera as steady as you can.

KEEPING YOUR CAMERA STEADY

The way you hold your camera will greatly affect your picture taking and make the difference between a pin sharp picture and a blurred picture caused by camera shake. The following will assist in taking sharp pictures:

- Grip the camera firmly with the right hand, finger positioned on the button. The left hand should be placed under the lens barrel. Being held like this, you should be able to remove either hand and still have a tight grip on the camera.

• Stand or sit in a position where you will not sway about, use a support to lean against, especially when using slow shutter speeds. Keep your elbows tucked into your body for support.

• Hold your breath, squeeze the shutter and breathe out.

• Use a faster shutter speed whenever practically possible.

• If shooting from a vehicle, turn the engine off.

METERING

We have discussed how the cameras' meter is able to read the amount of light and adjust the settings accordingly to obtain the correct exposure. Metering systems vary from camera to camera but most modern cameras work on 'Multi Pattern' metering. The cameras 'eye' is split into separate individual 'cells', the cameras computer then averages the amount of light read in each of these cells to give a suitable reading.

Many cameras have a Spot Metering area which helps when shooting in difficult situations.

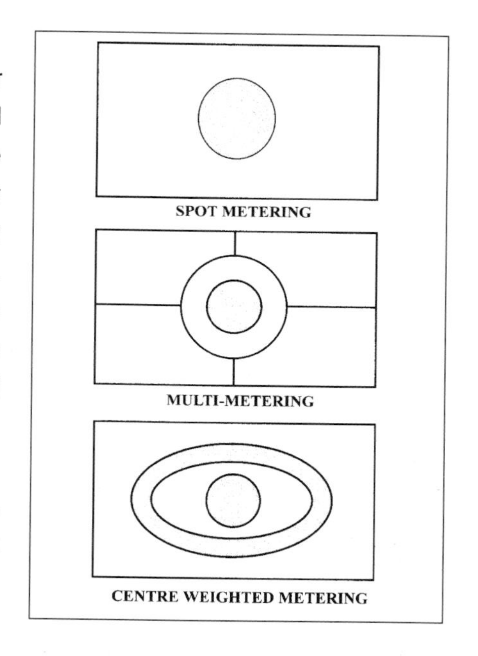

SPOT METERING

If your camera has a spot metering facility you will find this may be one of the most important features when taking covert photographs, to obtain a correct exposure.

This meter is very precise where only the light at the centre of the lens is measured.

When the 'spot' button is pressed, the metering system restricts its measurement to the small circular area marked in the viewfinder frame. Therefore any light outside this area is ignored.

So why is this of use to surveillance photography when there is a great deal of contrast in the surroundings? e.g.

- **When your subject is dark, surrounded by bright features**
- **When your subject is bright surrounded by dark features**

Surroundings too bright
If we have to take a photograph of a man who is stood in front of a white garage door loading a white van, the cameras' meter would normally read all of this 'whiteness' and close down the aperture to obtain an average exposure.

In doing so, the man will turn out very dark and under exposed. With spot metering, the spot is placed over the image of the man and the photo taken. The meter reads only the light off the man ensuring a correct exposure.

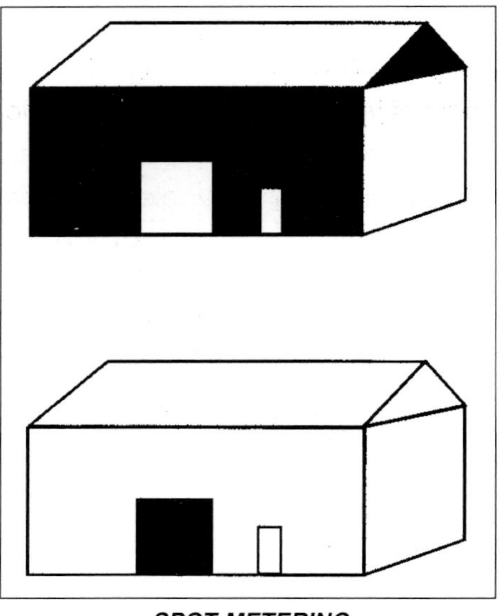

SPOT METERING

A similar situation would occur when your Subject is stood in front of a bright window, in snow or when the sun is behind him, giving him a silhouette.

Surroundings too dark
Additionally if you are shooting into a garage in poor light but the inside of the garage is illuminated, a normal exposure would read the 'dark' areas and so open the aperture to obtain an average exposure. In doing this, the man would appear bright and over exposed. Again, the spot would be placed over the Subject and the photo taken ensuring that the Subject is correctly exposed.

If your camera does not have a spot metering facility and you find yourself taking photographs in similar conditions, you may be able to adjust your camera manually by over-exposing or under-exposing the picture by 1 or 2 stops (f numbers). Care should be used when using the exposure override control so that you do not compensate the wrong way. **If the surroundings are too bright - over expose, if they are too dark - under expose.**

LENSES

The lens is the device which focuses the light on to the film to form an image, unless that image is sharp you will not produce clear pictures.

FOCAL LENGTH

The angle of view photographed by any lens is governed by its focal length (usually measured in millimetres), which is the distance from the lens to the film.

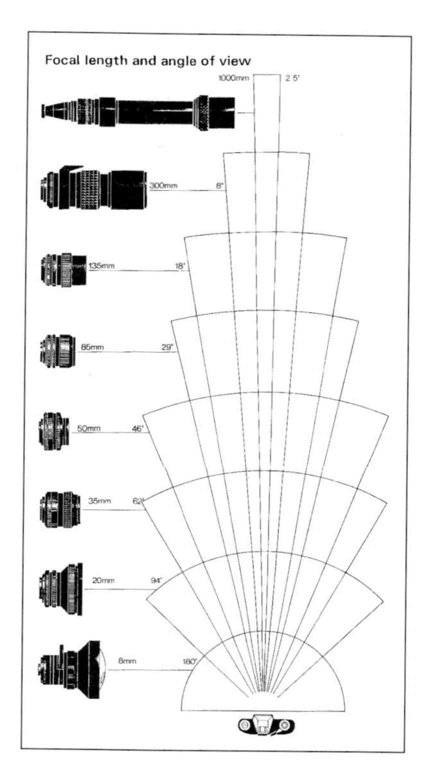

Focal length and angle of view

On a 35mm camera a standard lens (50 mm) has roughly the same view as the human eye. To photograph more of a wider area, or to bring a Subject closer you will need lenses of a different focal length.

RANGE OF LENSES

There are a wide range of lenses available and to the surveillance photographer, lenses of 300mm, (telephoto), are normally adequate to bring your Subject in close enough.

Zoom lenses, (lenses with varying focal length such as 28-70mm, 70-210 or 100-300m), are ideal and they enable you to frame the picture.

LENS SPEED

As previously mentioned, a large aperture will let in more light than a smaller aperture. Lens size is relative to how large that aperture may be. For example an average 50mm lens will have an aperture range of **f1.4-f16** whereas an average 300mm lens will have an aperture range of **f4.5-f22.** This **f** number is referred to as the speed of the lens, dictating how fast it is.

This tells us that the 300mm lens will not be able to cope with poor light conditions only having its widest aperture of **f4.5** instead of **f1.4.** Fast 300mm/f2.8 lenses are available as are 800mm/f2.8 lenses but they are very expensive. These fast lenses are also quite large in size and can often be seen being used by the Paparazzi and sports photographers.

TELE-CONVERTERS

Tele-converters offer a cheap way of extending your lens by increasing the focal length of the lens that you already have. A tele-converter is a small cylindrical tube which is fitted between the camera and the lens. A 2x converter doubles the focal length so that a 200mm telephoto becomes a more powerful 400mm.

The main disadvantages of tele-converters is that your aperture settings will be reduced by **2 f** stops and will not let in as much light, i.e. if your 300mm lens is **f4** it now becomes **f8** and so shooting in low light may be difficult.

A mirror lens is a telephoto, usually with a focal length of 500mm. They utilise internal mirrors to fold light to enable the lens to be as short and as lightweight as possible, (approx 5 inches long) The only drawback is that they usually have a fixed aperture, (normally **f8**) which can be limiting in poor light.

FOCUSING

There is nothing worse than having a photograph that is out of focus. Auto-focus cameras are now as common as manual focus cameras. They offer speed, ease of handling and also have the facility to be operated manually. They also offer continuous auto-focusing which will 'track' an approaching car for example.

MANUAL FOCUSING

Various techniques can be used when manual focusing is required.

- **PREDICTIVE FOCUSING**

  If you know that your Subject is going to pass a certain point, (such as a car emerging from a gate), focus on that point and wait for your Subject to appear. You may want to apply a piece of masking tape to the lens barrel in order to hold the focusing ring firm. This way you will not accidentally knock the camera out of focus.

• FOLLOW FOCUSING

If your Subject is moving then you will have to continually adjust the focus with your left hand as the Subject moves. This technique can be tricky and requires practice. Maximum depth of field should be used if at all possible.

TYPES OF FILM

Using the correct film for the right situation can make all the difference between a good and a bad picture. It is therefore vitally important to know about the full range of films available.

There are many brands of film available and they vary in price. If you keep to brand names such as Fuji, Kodak or Ilford, you should not experience any problems of quality. Experience will help you decide which is the best to use.

When choosing a film decide on:

- Colour or Monochrome.
- Film Speed.
- Number of Exposures (24 or 36).
- Print or transparency (slides).

• MONOCHROME FILM

Black and white pictures, if taken properly, provide a good medium. If you do your own processing, it is possible to take photographs even when your exposure meter tells you that it is too dark. By using a technique called 'Uprating' and with a 400 ASA (ISO) film, you manually set the film speed to 800 ASA, (this gives you an extra **f** stop or lets you double your shutter speed), and is an important factor in low light situations.

When the film is processed the development time is increased to compensate for being under-exposed. Your processor should be informed of any uprating to make adjustments in developing.

The processing of monochrome film can often take over a week to be returned, but Ilford XP2 film can be processed at any high street processors in an hour. The only disadvantage is that the prints turn out with a slight blue or pink tinge to them.

• COLOUR FILM

Colour print film is probably the film that you would use on most occasions. It comes in many different speeds, (explained later), and can be processed within an hour at many high street photo shops.

• INFRA RED - HIGH SPEED FILM

Infra Red film is available and enables photographs to be taken in total darkness and is explained later in the chapter.

CARE OF FILM

The following points should be noted:

Film date	When you buy film, check it is not out of date.
Avoid heat	Film deteriorates in warm conditions. If you keep a stock, the refrigerator shelf is ideal or somewhere cool.
Loading	Always load and unload film in dull or dark conditions. Make sure the film and internal parts of the camera are free from dust and dirt.
Jammed film	If your film is jammed and will not wind on, open the cameras' back in a darkened room and try to rectify the problem.
Used film	Always wind the film right back into the cassette to prevent accidental re-loading. Have it processed as soon as possible.

FILM SPEED

The term 'Film Speed' describes how 'light sensitive' a film is. A 'fast' film reacts very fast to light. A 'slow' film is less sensitive to light, it reacts slower and therefore requires brighter light conditions or a longer exposure.

GRAINY PHOTOGRAPHS

Film is made up of light sensitive crystals. It is the size and number of these crystals, which determine the film speed. The crystals, (or grains) on fast film are much larger than those on slow film, which is why fast film produces 'grainier' pictures. A slower film such as 100ASA will provide a high resolution photograph.

SPEED RATINGS

Film is usually marked with two speed ratings ISO/ASA, (International/American), or DIN, (German). ASA/ISO is much more commonly used and we use this in our examples.

The table shows various speeds for colour film and their common uses.

SPEED	ASA/ISO	USE
SLOW	(25) (50) (64)	Static Subject requiring detai landscapes, buildings, studio work, portraits etc.
MEDIUM	(100) (125) (200)	General use.
FAST	(400) (800)	Sports, Action, Low light, Surveillance.
HIGH SPEED	(1000) (1600) (3200)	Low light surveillance.

- **SLOW SPEED FILM**

  Slow film gives sharp detail and a grain free image. It is an ideal film for static Subjects such as landscapes, buildings or still life. It requires longer exposure times and therefore has little use in surveillance photography.

- **MEDIUM SPEED FILM**

  This is the best for general purpose photography and gives a compromise between speed and grain. You may get away with using medium film if the light is good or you are using a 'fast' lens.

- **FAST AND HIGH SPEED FILM**

  These films are a must for surveillance photography, especially speeds of ASA 400, 800 or 1000 ASA.

  In low light they give you the ability to shoot at faster shutter speeds, (avoiding camera shake with long lenses). In bright light they perform equally as well. As previously mentioned, high speed film means that pictures look grainy, but with speeds of 800 and 1000 the results are acceptable. Manufacturers are continually improving film and it is possible that in a couple of years 1000 ASA will have the resolution of 100 ASA film.

SETTING FILM SPEED

Once you have loaded your film, the film speed should be set on the cameras speed dial. Whenever you load a new film, always check this dial. A wrong setting may cause your pictures to be incorrectly exposed.

DX FILMS

The majority of all films are now 'DX coded'. This code is a type of bar code found on the film cassette and most modern cameras have a DX reading facility. With this facility, the camera automatically sets the film speed on loading rather than having to do it manually with a dial.

REMOVING A FILM FOR LATER USE

If you only take eight pictures on one roll of film and then wish to remove it so it can be reloaded at a later date, this can be easily done. Make a note of how many exposures you have made and then rewind the film into its cartridge leaving out the 'leader'. Write the number of pictures taken on this to act as a reminder.

When you need to reload the film again, do so as you would normally. Fit a cap onto the lens and keep the camera in darkness in the event the cap is loose fitting. Set the shutter speed to a fast setting and run off the required number of frames to get you back to the right place where the last picture was taken, (eight in this case). Then take another two frames in the event the frames overlap. Should you have a Data Back fitted, make sure this is switched off otherwise a time/date will appear on each on the eight photographs.

PHOTOGRAPHIC COMPOSITION

Far too often photographers do not maximise the picture frame, to film their Subject. Attempt to cram in as much of the scene as possible and use the whole frame so the Subject is not lost.

ADVANCED PHOTOGRAPHIC TECHNIQUES

PANORAMIC PHOTOGRAPHS

Quite often you may be required to take a Panoramic photograph if the premises or scene covers a wide area. Rather than use a wide angle lens, a telephoto should be used in order to photograph detail

The picture is made by taking a series of photographs and then panning the camera slightly after each shot is taken. The resulting photographs are then joined together to form an overall wide picture. It is important to hold the camera so that it pans horizontally and a tripod could be used here. Take the series of pictures from left to right, each one just overlapping the last. This overlap assists in lining them up and joining them together after printing.

AERIAL PHOTOGRAPHY

There may be occasions when you will be required to take an aerial photograph giving you a birds eye view of your Subject, particularly when carrying out a reconnaissance.

To hire a photographer who specialises in aerial work can be quite costly, these photographers are normally pilots who have an interest in photography and use this combination to earn a living by providing commercial and private clients with pictures. If you already know a pilot you are half way to obtaining your photographs. Photographs should be taken from as low as the pilot will allow, taking into consideration that you may not want to alert the Subject.

The following should be considered:

- Brief your pilot in advance, he may need weather reports and flight clearance for certain areas. He will want to know estimates of flying time in order to calculate fuel consumption which affects costs.

- Use a medium speed film to provide picture quality.
- Use a fast shutter speed of 1/500 second or more as the aircraft will vibrate.
- Try to support the camera to avoid camera shake.

- Use a lens hood to prevent 'flare' from the sun.
- Set focus to Infinity.
- If the light is bright, use an Ultra Violet (U.V.) filter.
- Use a motordrive - take as many shots as possible, it could be costly to make a second flight.
- Avoid shooting early or late in the day, if the sun is bright it will cause long shadows.
- Use an aeroplane as opposed to a helicopter. They are quieter, cheaper, plentiful and less observed from the ground.

PHOTOGRAPHING TELEVISION SCREENS

You may need to obtain hard copies of a scene that has been shot on video. This can be done with the aid of a video printer, especially designed for the purpose, or by using special software, (video capture), on a personal computer. Alternatively you can photograph the T.V. screen which can easily be done if carried out properly.

Set your camera on a tripod fitted with a lens of about 100mm in front of your T.V or monitor and fill the frame with the screen. A shutter release cable should ideally be used to avoid any camera shake. Darken the room as much as possible, this enables the correct exposure to be read from the screen and avoids reflections off the screen from windows. Adjust the picture controls for sharpness and contrast.

The T.V picture you see on the screen is made up of ever-changing tiny dots which replace each other every 1/30th of a second and so create a moving picture. Should the screen be photographed at a fast shutter speed, a dark band may appear across the photograph and ruin the picture. For this reason a slow shutter speed is required, so set the shutter to either 1/15th or even better 1/8th of a second and let your camera's meter select the correct aperture.

Should the T.V screen be curved, try to make use of depth of field so that the edges of the screen are not out of focus, and focus on the centre of the screen.

INFRA-RED PHOTOGRAPHY

When it is necessary to take photographs in darkness, you would normally use a conventional flash to provide the light source. For covert reasons this may not always be practical or tactical as the light from the flash will alert others to your presence. The power of flash, even though for a fraction of a second is very powerful and can be seen over great distances.

The use of Infra Red film combined with an Infra Red light source, (such as a flash), will enable you to take photographs in complete darkness, undetected.

Infra Red Film

Infra red film is available from most good photographic dealers and costs about £6.00 for a roll of 36 exposures, processing is not more than £10.00 and Kodak or Konica film is the easiest to obtain. The film is in either colour slide, or monochrome print format, I would recommend the use of the mono print film as the colour film produces odd colours (this film is mainly used for scientific purposes).

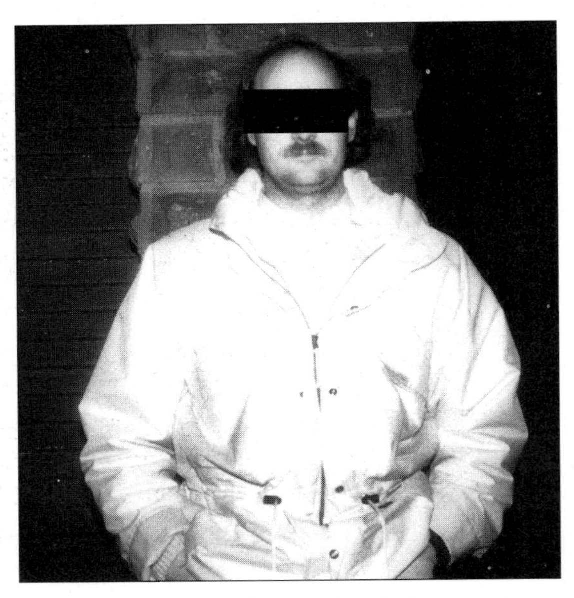

This photo was taken in complete darkness using infra-red film and flash. For the photographers amongst you - ISO 125 was set and taken at 125th sec. at F5.6.

The film should be handled with care and be removed from its plastic container and loaded into the camera in **COMPLETE** darkness. Likewise when the film is removed from the camera and put back into its container it should also be done in darkness.

The exposed film can be processed by many major film processors although it may take a week or so to be returned. For the DIY darkroom technician, the film is developed in D76 chemicals and then printed as normal. The developing has to take place in total darkness, which means that no red 'darkroom lights' can be used. As with any black and white negatives you are able to have prints made from them at any high street processors, although the results will not be true monochrome but will have a light blue or sepia tint to them.

Once the film is loaded, set your cameras ASA/ISO meter to 100. The film is not speed rated and so any setting could be used but 100 should suffice.

Now your camera is loaded with infra red film all that is required is an infra red light source. This can be obtained by fitting a piece of infra red filter glass over your flash head.

Infra red glass is sold in small sheets from security specialists (to be fitted to lamps used for CCTV cameras). The glass is actually strong plastic which is dark red in colour and can be cut with a hack-saw and filed to shape.

This picture was taken in total darkness using infra-red film and flash.

Some flash heads have a recess at the front to accommodate special effects filters. If your flash is of similar design you can shape your I.R filter to fit tightly in this space. It should then be held in place with black insulating tape, to cut out any escaping light through possible gaps.

When the flash is fired in darkness you will not see any light (but it is there), in an invisible form, as it is infra red. What may be seen, is a pink flash if you look directly into the flash head.

Your camera will need to be used in 'manual mode' so that the correct settings are obtained. As a guide, a shutter speed of 1/60th at an aperture of f5.6 or f8 will be needed. I would recommend that you experiment with this film if you have not used it before and 'bracket' the exposures, i.e. a speed of 1/60th but aperture set to f2.8, f5.6, or f8 to obtain the desired setting.

- **Focusing**

Infra red light focuses differently to that of normal light and on some lens barrels you will find a red dot which is used for this purpose. The distance from your camera to the Subject is normally set on the scale detailed on the lens. Infra red pictures require the distance to be set to the red dot which is slightly off centre.

If your lens does not have a red I.R dot then it would be wise to focus at a point that is a few feet behind the Subject to be photographed. A wide angle lens such as a 20mm or 28mm is preferred with Infra Red photography to provide a maximum depth of field and also enables you to photograph objects close up and obtain detail such as documents etc.

PHOTOGRAPHIC ACCESSORIES

TRIPODS

The best way to prevent camera shake is by the use of some support such as a tripod, other alternatives are:

Monopod One legged tripod.

'G' clamp Which can be attached to almost any surface with a fitting for the camera.

Bean bag This small soft cushion will support and mould a camera in the correct position.

When using a tripod, a cable release should ideally be used to prevent touching the camera, causing it to shake.

CAMERA DATA BACKS

12-6-98
08-42

The back door of most SLR cameras can be replaced with a 'Data Back'. This enables the date and time to be printed onto your photograph as it is taken.

If using a Data Back ensure that the clock is synchronised correctly. A photograph with an incorrect time on it could be disadvantageous if it is to be used in legal proceedings, especially if they do not marry up with your log or other photographs/video recording.

LENS FILTERS

Effect filters have no place in surveillance photography. However, I would recommend fitting a skylight 1B filter to each of your lenses. This will give a slightly better colour rendition to your photographs but more importantly it will protect the front of your lens. It is far easier and cheaper to replace a scratched or cracked filter than it is to replace an expensive lens.

MOTOR DRIVES / AUTO WINDERS

Most modern auto focus cameras have a built in 'autowinder' which automatically winds the film onto the next frame as a picture is taken. Non auto focus cameras can be fitted with a Motor Drive and this will enable you to take up to 5 frames per second, which is useful if your Subject is in view for only a short period.

In addition, they also give you the opportunity to take a series of photographs without having to move the camera away from your eye whilst winding on the film. This not only enables you to view your Subject constantly but also minimises camera shake.

COMPACT CAMERAS

There are many compact cameras available and these are handy for their small size and simplicity of use. Although their lenses cannot be interchanged, some have a built-in zoom lens of 35-110mm. They are auto-focus and can be fitted with a Data Back. These cameras can easily be concealed in a pocket and can be produced quickly to take a no fuss photograph using built in flash if required.

POINTS WHEN CHOOSING A CAMERA

1. Ask an experienced user for their recommendation, rather than take a Camera Sales Persons' advice.
2. Choose a camera that will withstand knocks and rough handling.
3. Choose lenses with focal length and speed in mind, 100-300mm is ideal. The two lenses that I use as standard are a 28-70mm and a 100-300mm.
4. Make sure the camera feels comfortable in your hands and is well balanced.
5. Are the controls simple and quick to use?
6. Does it have a Spot metering facility?
7. Does it have various exposure modes?
8. Operating the camera may appear complicated at first, after a few days of handling and practise, you will soon become accustomed to it

PHOTOGRAPHIC TIPS

- Hold the camera steady - use a support if necessary.
- Use a fast shutter speed when shooting hand held, especially with a telephoto lens.
- Use a high speed film in low light.
- Use 'spot metering' or adjust exposure if necessary in contrasting light conditions.
- Maximise use of depth of field when possible.

VIDEO PHOTOGRAPHY

Video cameras have become so small that they can easily fit into the palm of your hand. Most models available have pretty much the same features and will vary in price due to their size and the amount of extra features they have.

The latest style of Camcorder incorporates a 'Night Vision' facility which is able to record pictures in total darkness, (or zero lux). The camera can be switched from daylight mode to night mode quite simply and only infra red light, (which is invisible to the naked eye), will be recorded. Built into the camera are a number of infra red light emitting diodes (LED's) which illuminate the area to the front of the camera with 'invisible' light.

There are certain features to look for in a video camera when using it for surveillance. A good brand name such as Sony, JVC or Panasonic should give you a quality camera and the following features are essential:

- Minimum of a 12 x Zoom lens (Optical).
- Anti-Shake Feature.
- Ability to playback through the viewfinder or screen.
- Manual focus as well as auto focus.
- Time and date facility.
- Standard and slow recording speeds - which double your recording time.
- Back light compensator to avoid under exposure.

It is worthwhile obtaining a text book on video photography from your local library. Video photography is not always easy and your films can be greatly improved just by learning a few simple techniques concerning panning, zooming and composition. All of which enhance your film making it more professional.

Camera shake is more apparent when using video, especially when filming at the top end of your zoom. Whenever possible use a support such as a tripod. If possible get in closer to your Subject and hold the camera with both hands.

Camera shake is the main fault when using video and is very distracting to watch.

Most cameras, (Camcorders), have an auto focus lens, care should be used when in this mode. The majority of filming should be done in the manual focus mode for more control. When the camera is pointed at the Subject (let's say on the other side of a busy street) and a car or pedestrian pass between you and the Subject. The camera will automatically focus on the person passing by until he has left the viewfinder, after which, the lens will re-focus on your Subject.

This can be annoying if the area is busy and will result in the film shot being continually in and out of focus.

Sound (Audio)

Many surveillances requiring video evidence do not require audio on the tape, unless voices or certain sounds need to be heard as part of that evidence.

It would be wise to insert a dummy plug into the external microphone socket, (if the camera has one). This disables the built in microphone and avoids recording any unwanted sounds whilst you are filming such as radio voice procedure, background noises/voices etc.

PORTABLE COVERT CCTV CAMERAS

Covert Close Circuit T.V. and video has an important role in covert evidence gathering. By means of a video camera linked to a video recorder and monitor you will be able to watch unobtrusively, events taking place at the time they happen or view them at a later date.

Many cameras have been installed and supplied in the past which have achieved excellent results, especially where theft and unauthorised access to premises have been suspect. If the problem can be resolved by covert cameras it saves much manpower, time and unnecessary expense having to provide a manned observation team. In addition a covert camera maybe the only option available to you if the target area is impossible to watch.

During one investigation, we were required to video a number of meetings that took place in a company directors office, in a matter involving fraud. The office was well decorated and tidy with nothing on the walls where we could conceal a camera.

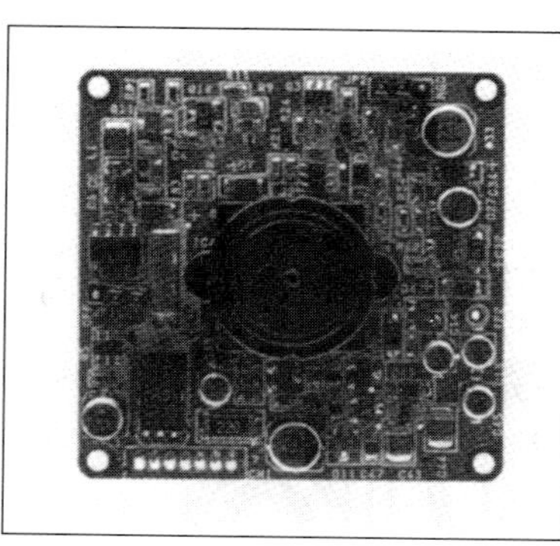

A miniature, pinhole monochrone camera which provides a very crisp, 380 - line resolution picture.

It was decided that the camera was to be buried in a plaster partitioned wall, with the cable running up though the partition and over the ceiling. To mount the camera we soaked away the decorative wall paper border and set the camera into the plasterboard. The border was then pasted back onto the wall and a tiny hole was cut into it for the 'pin hole' lens. A microphone was similarly installed and we were able to video record all that was said and done in the Subjects office.

Hardware

Cameras are now available on the security market that are as small as a matchbox and are as thin as a wafer. A camera such as this can be concealed in almost any object and placed in a position to view the target area. The camera may be able to be fitted with several lenses, which will give you a choice of a wide angle or telephoto views.

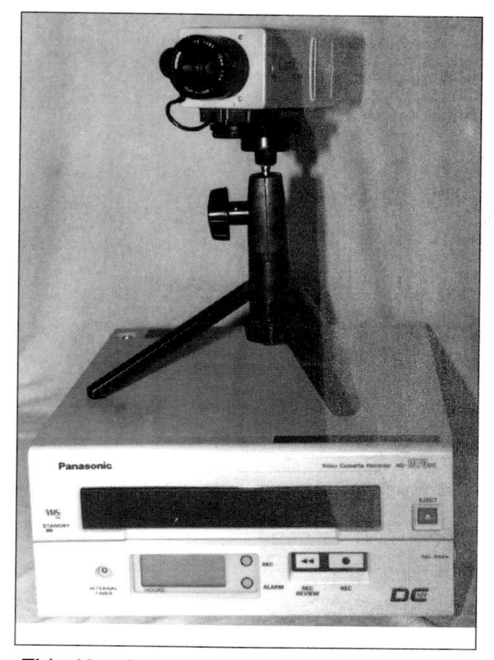

This 12 volt camera and time-lapse video recorder, will operate for 24 hours from a single car battery.

The camera will normally require a power source (normally 12 Volts), and a cable for the video signals. Four core telephone cable to link cameras to the recorder, is ideal for short runs.

A standard domestic video recorder will provide you with a maximum of eight hours record time when set at slow speed. Any longer recording time required and you will have to resort to a Time Lapse Recorder. These recorders are more expensive than your standard machines but can record for periods of anything from 3 to 960 hours on a standard VHS tape. In addition the time lapse VCR will print the time and date onto the recording.

Video Transmission Systems.

If your camera cannot be physically connected to your video recorder by cable, it is possible to transmit the video signal by radio waves to a receiver which in turn is connected to your video recorder. Obviously the camera and video transmitter will still require a power supply but no other cables would be necessary.

This system is useful should you want to place a covert camera on the parcel shelf of a vehicle which has been parked outside the Subjects premises in order to 'trigger' the surveillance. With the camera pointing in the direction of a doorway or at a car, you will be able to sit some distance away and view the area under observation by means of a T.V monitor.

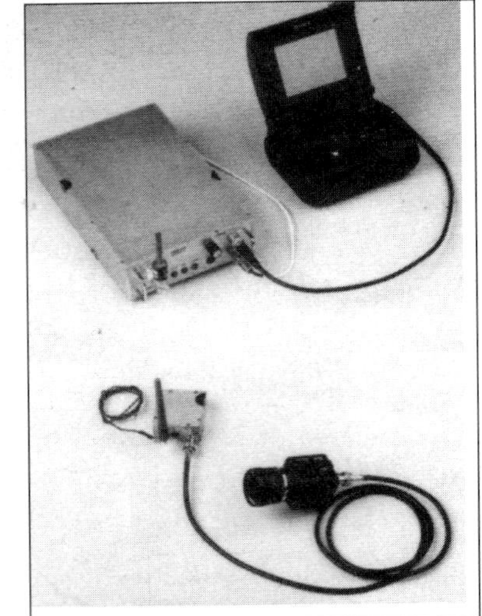

This system has been used in the past when the Subject address was extremely difficult to observe and it was not possible to 'trigger' the Subject leaving by normal means. A camera and a video transmitter, (together with a car battery), were buried in a hedgerow opposite the Subject's property. An operator was then able to sit some 400 metres away and observe the property by means of a small T.V. monitor.

He was able to put the team on 'standby' and give the direction of the Subject when he departed.

PORTABLE COVERT VIDEO CAMERAS

These camera systems can be purchased or be put together yourself with some technological know how. The cameras can be housed in carriers such as a briefcase, handbag, jacket or a sports bag.

Using a very small video recorder and connected to a pinhole lens, the system is small and portable enough for you to make covert video recordings. The system can be taken into meetings, or areas that you want to record secretly.

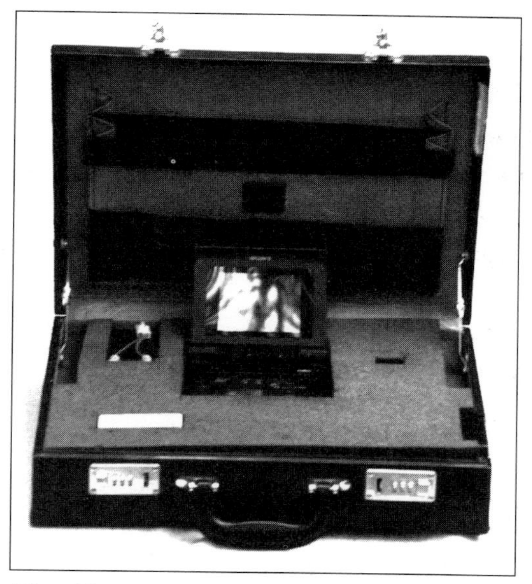

The video briefcase. The recording unit and power system can easily be transferred to operate in a sports bag or handbag.

These systems are invaluable when carrying out 'personal injury' type investigations, especially when following the Subject on foot. You do not always have to face or be behind the Subject, in order to film him, if your camera is housed in a sports bag for example, you could be 'side on' to him or even in front of the Subject with the lens pointing in the right direction.

On one personal injury investigation, the Subject was followed to a local sports centre where she joined a class doing step aerobics. The camera, (in a sports bag) was left on the floor of the gym unattended and left to do the 'work'.

On another occasion, the Subject was followed to an Italian restaurant where he worked as a waiter. With some quick thinking we put the camera system in a small cardboard box obtained from a nearby supermarket. The box was then wrapped in gift wrapping paper and a tiny hole was made for the lens. The two operators then went into the restaurant for a meal, the 'present' was placed on the table between them and video film was obtained of the waiter carrying out his duties.

The subject caught going shopping.

GLOSSARY OF TERMS

GLOSSARY OF TERMS USED IN VOICE PROCEDURE

EXPRESSION TO BE USED	MEANING OF EXPRESSION
ADVANCE WARNING	Given in the text of 'Advance Warning - traffic lights, the lights are at red', or 'Advance Warning 'T' junction', etc.
BACK UP	Second vehicle in the convoy, supporting Eyeball.
BUS REQUEST	To be used instead of the term 'Bus Stop' in order to eliminate confusion.
CANCEL MY LAST	Ignore my last message.
CLICK & DOUBLE CLICK	When an operator cannot speak on the air a series of clicks are made by pressing the radios PTT switch. i.e one click for 'NO' and two clicks for 'YES'. A series of clicks can mean a warning, such as Standby.
COME THROUGH	Given after 'Hang Back' to bring convoy through.
COMMITTED, COMMITTED	Means the target is committed to still travel on a motorway.
COMPLETE	Returned or Inside. e.g. 'India Complete' indicates that call sign India has returned to his vehicle after he has been on foot. Also used to indicate when a person has entered a building etc.

CONTACT, CONTACT.	Indicates Eyeball is regained by one of the vehicles in the convoy, following search procedure. Point of contact is relayed to the team specifying direction and speed of target.
CONTINUING STRAIGHT.	Used when the Subject is committed to the same road without any deviation.
CONVOY.	All vehicles comprising the surveillance team.
C.T.R.	Close Target Recce. Where operators conduct a close examination of a target premises.
EYEBALL.	Vehicle or Operative having primary visual contact with the target and who is directing the operation for the time being.
EYEBALL REGAINED.	Indicates target again in view, following temporary loss.
FOXTROT.	When someone is walking they are referred to as going 'Foxtrot'.
GO AHEAD.	A request made to pass a message.The single term "GO" should not be used as it is too easily confused with "NO". The word SEND has the same meaning.
GOING ROUND AGAIN.	Indicates that the target vehicle is commencing a second, or subsequent, circuit of a roundabout. Thereafter, the commentary will continue as for the first circuit, in relation to the exits he does or does not take.
GONE.	Indicating movement, i.e. 'Gone Left Left Left.'

HANDLING.	The person driving a vehicle is said to be 'Handling'.
HANG BACK.	Transmission from Eyeball, indicating to convoy that they should 'hang back' as the target vehicle is slowing and may stop.
HELD.	Used when there is a temporary stop, ie. waiting at a red light.
INTENDING.	Indicates in which direction the Subject is pointing or intending to move or likely to travel.
LEFT, LEFT, LEFT.	Indicates that the target vehicle has turned left.
MANOEUVRING.	Warning issued by Eyeball, indicating that the target vehicle is,manoeuvring in a par park or the road etc.
MAKE GROUND.	Instruction from Eyeball to another vehicle in the convoy to get in a position to accept the "eyeball" where required.
NEARSIDE, OFFSIDE INDICATION.	States nearside/offside indicator is operating on the Subject vehicle.
NO DEVIATION.	Indicates target vehicle is continuing straight ahead, as at a crossroads. NOT to be used on motorways.
NOT ONE, NOT TWO ETC.	Indicates that the target vehicle negotiating a round-about has passed first, second exit etc. 'No Entry' roads are not counted as exits.
OFF, OFF, OFF.	Transmission by Eyeball, indicating that the target is now on the move. MOBILE is also used as a substitute.
ONE UP, TWO UP, ETC.	Indicating the amount of people in a vehicle.

ORIGINAL.	The term used when the target has resumed moving after a stop and is continuing in the Original (same) direction prior to the stop.
OPTION.	Indicates a possible turning or route that the Subject can take. i.e. '2nd Option on the nearside'.
OUT, OUT, OUT.	Indicates that the target is alighting from a vehicle or is leaving premises.
PERMISSION.	Where an operator asks Eyeball for 'Permission' to interrupt the commentary to pass on a message. Commentary should not be interrupted without Permission.
RADIO CHECK.	Request to test communications with the remainder of the team. Call signs should respond in alphabetical order.
RECEIVED.	Used to acknowledge a message. ROGER can also has the same meaning.
RECIPROCAL.	Indicates that target has done a 'U' turn and is returning along the same route. May be abbreviated to 'RECIP'.
RIGHT, RIGHT, RIGHT.	Indicates that target vehicle has turned right.
SHADOW CAR(S).	Vehicle being used to back up a footman.
SHOWN OUT.	If an operator is compromised they have 'shown out'.
SO FAR	When the transmitting long messages, the term "So Far" is used to break up a message.

STAND DOWN.	Indicates cancellation of whole operation.
STOP, STOP, STOP.	Indicates that target vehicle has stopped in circumstances other than a 'held' situation.
STRIKE, STRIKE, STRIKE.	Indicates designated operators will move in and effect arrest or searches etc.
STANDBY, STANDBY	Instruction issued by Eyeball or Trigger, alerting the team to possible movement of the Subject.
SUBJECT	Person Subject of the surveillance. Target may also be used.
SUBJECT HELD.	Indicates temporary stop by target vehicle, and will normally be followed by an explanation for that stop, i.e. traffic lights, pedestrian crossing, traffic congestion etc.
TAIL END CHARLIE.	Rearmost vehicle in convoy.
TAKEN FIRST, TAKEN SECOND ETC.	Indicates that target vehicle has taken first, second, etc., exit off roundabout.
TRIGGER.	Term used for Eyeball when the Eyeball has to trigger or start the surveillance.
TEMPORARY LOSS.	Indicates a temporary loss of Eyeball, due to terrain, traffic or other conditions.
TOTAL LOSS.	Indicates Eyeball not regained following temporary loss. A total loss will normally be followed by a pre-planned search procedure.
UNSIGHTED.	Indicates that the Subjected is out of your view.

VISUAL. Used to indicate that an operator has a view of the target, vehicle, home address, cafe etc., i.e. "India has B1 Visual". Sometimes abbreviated to, "I have".

WAIT. Used to indicate that operators should not transmit for the time being and to wait for further transmissions.

The normal radio term "STAND BY" has a clearly defined meaning within surveillance and this should never be used instead of 'Wait'.

T.K. Abbreviated - Telephone Kiosk.

P.H. Abbreviated - Public House.

H.A. Abbreviated - Home Address.

Identifier Codes

A **male** is referred to as an **ALPHA**.

A **vehicle** is referred to as a **BRAVO.**

A **property,** such as a house or building, is a **CHARLIE.**

A **female** is referred to as an **ECHO.**

FURTHER SOURCES OF INFORMATION

SURVEILLANCE TEAMS AND SECURITY CONSULTANCY

Highly experienced, professional and fully equipped surveillance teams provided for Commercial and Corporate Investigations and Personal Injury Investigations. Offering a National and Worldwide service to Legal and Corporate bodies.

SURVEILLANCE TRAINING COURSES

Offering a 4-Day basic techniques course covering the subjects contained in this book. Taught by experienced and qualified instructors, the course offers realistic and practical training exercises. 'In-House' training or residential courses are catered for and courses can be tailored to suit individual or agency requirements.

TRAINING

COVERT ELECTRONIC SURVEILLANCE SYSTEMS

Professional mains & battery-operated Room Transmitters, Telephone Transmitters & Telephone Intercepts. Receivers, Recorders & Counter Surveillance Equipment. Covert Video Recording Systems & Satellite Vehicle Tracking Systems.

CONTACT: THE SPY SHOP
365 Kirkstall Road
Leeds
West Yorkshire LS4 2HQ

Tel: 0113 230 2000
Fax: 0113 230 2030
web: www.spyshop.co.uk

THE SPY SHOP

CLOSE PROTECTION (BODYGUARD) TRAINING

Basic, Intermediate & Advanced training courses in this specialised field of security. The subjects covered involve: Duties of a CPO, Unarmed Combat, First Aid, Threat Assessments, Anti-Surveillance, Communications, Kidnap Prevention, Tactical Driving, Terrorist Tactics, Weapons Skills & CQB and Crisis Management.

CONTACT: CHASE CONSULTANTS LTD
Unit 51, Chel Business Centre,
26 Roundhay Road,
Leeds, West Yorkshire LS7 1AB

Tel: 0113 2443109
Fax: 0113 2341410
e-mail: chaseconsultants@csi.com
web: www.protection-publications.co.uk

Please mention ***'Covert Surveillance Techniques'*** when contacting the above organisations.